Lise Andreana, CFP

No More Mac 'n' Cheese!

The Real-World Guide to Managing Your Money for 20-Somethings

Self-Counsel Press
(a division of)
International Self-Counsel Press Ltd.
USA   Canada

Self-Counsel Press acknowledges the financial support of the Government of Canada through the Canada Book Fund (CBF) for our publishing activities.

Printed in Canada.

First edition: 2011

Library and Archives Canada Cataloguing in Publication

Andreana, Lise

    No more mac 'n cheese!: the real-world guide to managing your money for 20-somethings / Lise Andreana.

    ISBN 978-1-77040-090-0

    1. Young adults — Finance, Personal. 2. Finance, Personal. I. Title.

HG179.A63 2011   332.0240084'2   C2011-904550-8

Every effort has been made to obtain permission for quoted material. If there is an omission or error, the author and publisher would be grateful to be so informed.

Self-Counsel Press
(a division of)
International Self-Counsel Press Ltd.

Bellingham, WA   North Vancouver, BC
USA   Canada

Contents

Conclusion   153

Samples

Exercises

Quizzes

Notice to Readers

Laws are constantly changing. Every effort is made to keep this publication as current as possible. However, the author, the publisher, and the vendor of this book make no representations or warranties regarding the outcome or the use to which the information in this book is put and are not assuming any liability for any claims, losses, or damages arising out of the use of this book. The reader should not rely on the author or the publisher of this book for any professional advice. Please be sure that you have the most recent edition.

Note: The fees quoted in this book are correct at the date of publication. However, fees are subject to change without notice. For current fees, please check with the court registry or appropriate government office nearest you.

Prices, commissions, fees, and other costs mentioned in the text or shown in samples in this book probably do not reflect real costs where you live. Inflation and other factors, including geography, can cause the costs you might encounter to be much higher or even much lower than those we show. The dollar amounts shown are simply intended as representative examples.

Dedication

Thank you Dad, for you never told me what to do; you simply lived your life. You turned 95 years old the week this book was submitted. Watching you I learned how to wait until tomorrow for a better today; defend the underdog; that good manners are nothing more than a series of petty sacrifices; and a penny saved today has the power to fund an entire lifetime, maybe even that of our children.

With nothing more than a grade school education, you served your country in WWII, turned the $2,000 land grant from Veterans Affairs into a $150,000 investment, married, and raised ten children — all of whom have the benefit of a postsecondary education. You continue to live in your own home. You are loved by all of us and Mother, the woman who has stood by your side for more than 60 years. I am indebted to you.

Thank you for inspiring my life and the stories within these pages.

Clarence B. Kelland said it best: "He didn't tell me how to live; he lived, and let me watch him do it."

Acknowledgments

If you had asked me five years ago, I would have said the last thing I expected to do in my lifetime was write a book. With a flourishing career as a financial planner, there was little time to think about reaching out to the public. The fact that I can now add author to my CV is the result of the support and help of many.

To my patient and loving husband, Gerry Kowalchuk, whose retirement plans do not include me working at my computer for a large part of each day. His contribution to Chapter 14, "Buying a Home," was invaluable. His 40+ years working in the real estate sector made him a natural on the topic. Gerry, you are the love of my life, and I am indebted to you for so many reasons. Thank you.

Thanks to Lois Richardson who went out of her way to ensure my name and ideas came to the attention of Eileen Velthuis, Managing Editor, at Self-Counsel Press. Eileen, thank you for giving me the chance to bring my ideas on financial planning to a wider audience. Thanks to Tanya Lee Howe who edited the reams of rough data and raw ideas I supplied — you edited my ugly duckling of a manuscript into a book I can be proud of.

Thanks to my friends and family for letting me pick your brains for ideas, and for taking the time and interest to add your ideas to improve upon the final product.

Introduction

"Money is only a tool. It will take you wherever you wish, but it will not replace you as the driver."

Ayn Rand

* Read this book if you arrive home to find a FOR SALE sign on the lawn and your parents gleefully tell you they have decided to downsize to a condo and have listed the contents of your bedroom on Kijiji!

* Read this book if you are a high achiever between the ages of 17 and 29 and are looking for solid tips to secure your future happiness and financial well-being.

If you are a young adult who has recently left home, or is considering leaving the family home, this book is for you. This book is designed to help you make smart decisions with money now and through the next decade. In the next few days, months, and years, you will be making financial decisions that will define your future relationship with money. Whether you decide to go it alone or choose a life partner, this is the decade which will take you from the family basement into your first apartment, when you'll establish a career, balance a budget, set short-term to midterm financial goals, purchase a vehicle, and perhaps even buy your first home.

This book will help you plan your postsecondary education, begin a career, move from the family home, and find a financial coach to help you along the way. You will learn to set goals for the next decade, create an inventory of your assets and skills, and place a value on your career and the hidden benefits that can put thousands of dollars in your pocket. You will learn to build a budget, show your money who is boss, learn the difference between smart debt and dumb debt, and find tips for investing your savings. You will also receive tips for making your first real estate investment.

It is my observation that even a very small financial success at this stage of your life can multiply into solid financial security in the future. Did you know that just $100 a month in savings could grow to $56,251[1] over the next 20 years? What would you do with $56,000? If you wanted to make a down payment on a home in year ten, how much would your savings be worth? $19,854!

Note that mistakes made at this stage can take years to reverse. Debt incurred now to buy those new jeans or the latest video game can stay on your credit card for years in the form of outrageously high interest rate charges. Let's say you buy those jeans on your credit card for $60 and only pay the interest for the next 20 years: Your jeans will cost you in excess of $325!

This book is designed to help you make the smart choice each and every time. The chapters are laid out so you can read the book from cover to cover, or you can pick and choose the topics of interest to you on any given day. Feel free to jump ahead to the topic which interests you the most.

Having a financial plan allows you to be strategic. Financial planning is a systematic methodology for making decisions which bring you closer to your goals. Your goals will be unique to you; the methodology for achieving your goals, however, has been well developed over time.

There are three simple steps you can take right now to help you secure the future happiness and the financial security you want:

1. Read this book.

2. Use the enclosed exercises to develop a strategy for achieving your goals — then implement your unique strategy.

3. Review your goals and the progress you have made often to ensure you are on track. Revise your goals and actions as required.

I wish you the best of luck as you set out on the road to financial success!

---

[1] Assuming 7 percent rate of return

CHAPTER ONE

The Difference in Finances between the Baby Boomers and Gen Y

★ Read this if you are tired of hearing complaints about *your* generation's ability to grow up.

★ Read this if you wonder what the difference is between your parent's generation and yours.

Things are different today, and as a young adult, you may be starting your financial life plan later than your parents did. Many in your generation have delayed adulthood by five to seven years, compared to your parents' generation. The advantage for your generation is that you are better educated and often have the financial support of your families as you enter your career years. By carefully selecting educational goals, following a prudent course of action, avoiding debt where possible, and making a wise career choice, you will be well on your way to financial security.

1. The Evolution of Personal Finances

There appears to be a growing trend for young adults to stay in the family home longer and to return several times before finally launching on their own. How will delayed adulthood affect a person's future financial well-being?

As a financial advisor for the past 15 years, I have helped more than 1,200 clients. During that time I have had the privilege to work with retirees raised during the 1930s and 1940s, professional Boomers born during the 1950s and 1960s, and young professionals born during the 1970s and 1980s.

It has become clear to me that each year, today's "new young adult" seems to be farther and farther removed from the common-sense, prudent money principles exercised by clients who grew up during earlier and simpler times ranging from 1940 to 1965. Why is it that clients who raised families in a single-paycheck environment, earned less, had fewer resources, and were less educated, managed to pay off debt while still in their 40s? They saved more, spent prudently, and lived within their means to achieve financial well-being in time to retire. What has changed?

For those of you born after 1985, your parents are "ancient history." As far as you are concerned, they might as well be talking about the Big Bang theory! A little history lesson may be in order since much of the information we hold to be true about financial security, creating wealth, and retirement planning is based on the baby boom generation. Bear with me; upon examination you will find out why the rules that worked for the Boomer generation will not work for you. The following example gives an insight into why there is a difference between the generations' financial management.

Cassie has just turned 25 and will graduate next spring from her local university, with a major in journalism. She has been listening to her parents go on and on about how it was when they were growing up in the 1960s and 1970s. They tell her, "By the time we had reached the age of 25 we had already married and bought our first home."

Cassie is beginning to feel like a failure for being so far behind. Like many young adults, she still lives at home with her parents, has $20,000 in student debt like so many students[1], has yet to land a full-time job, and is a long way from finding the person she wants to marry. Rather than get into an argument, Cassie decides to use her newly learned interviewing skills to get her parents to talk about the "good old days." This way she will be able to compare their experiences as young adults to her own.

Here is what Cassie discovers. Her parents, Francesca and Cano, came from working-class backgrounds. Cassie's grandparents did not have the resources to

---

[1] The Financial Consumer Agency of Canada, "Youth Financial Literacy Study," www.fcac-acfc.gc.ca/eng/resources, (2008), accessed June 2011.

help fund their children's postsecondary education and, at that time, student loans were a relatively new thing. Cano and Francesca were high school sweethearts.

Upon graduating from high school at the beginning of the 1980s, and with no hope of going to university, Cano, who wished he could become an architect, became a plumber apprentice instead. Becoming an architect would have meant many more years of school with no money to pay for his education. Francesca went to teachers' college. Soon they were both working. Their employers provided benefits and pensions. Francesca and Cano may not *love* their work, but they are satisfied that their future offers financial security and they expect to retire at age 65 after 40 years of work.

A year after graduating from their programs, they had a big wedding. Cano and Francesca's parents hosted the wedding, the bride's parents paid for the reception, and the groom's family provided a cash gift of $1,000. The bridal shower provided the needs of the home from kitchen to bed and bath. Cash was also a popular wedding gift. The wedding provided Cano and Francesca with most of their household needs and a total of $2,000 in cash.

Soon after the wedding, Cano and Francesca found a home. Using the $2,000 savings from their wedding and adding another $5,000 they managed to save on their own, they were able to qualify for a mortgage on their dream home, a semi-detached dwelling in the suburbs.

Cassie and her parents feel good about their conversation. Francesca and Cano are sentimental and love talking about their life together. They are pleased Cassie is interested in understanding the sacrifices they made for the betterment of their family. Cassie now understands her parents sacrificed the education and the careers they would have preferred to enable them to marry and have a family, respectful of the social mores of the day.

Let's compare the lives of Cassie and that of her parents at age 25:

- Cano and Francesca at age 25 are newly married and both have new careers, an apartment full of new furniture, no debt, and a nest egg of $7,000 to help them make their first home purchase.

- Cassie, at age 25, is living in the family basement and is starting her career with a $20,000 debt.

She compares her $20,000 debt at age 25 with how her parents began with $7,000 in savings at age 25. Cano and Francesca married in 1985 so Cassie adjusts their age 25 starting point for inflation. The $7,000[2] start is equivalent to $14,000 today! That represents a $34,000 difference in net worth at age 25.

---

[2] Bureau of Labor Statistics, "Consumer Price Index," www.bls.gov/cpi, (2011), accessed June 2011.

Cassie has a good education in a field of her choosing. She has a promising future career which she expects will be personally fulfilling. Cassie and her peers have more choices, easy access to student loans, and credit cards.

Many young adults of today are better educated than their parents. Education takes time; this means that today's young adult is entering the job market later in life and more often is graduating with student loans and credit card debt.

Today's young adults are reluctant to accept a work environment in which they do not feel fulfilled. This is in stark contrast to their parents' generation who made career and financial sacrifices in their early years in order to have an easier life later. This generation of young adults is less prepared to make sacrifices and save a portion of today's income for a better life tomorrow. Is it any wonder today's graduating students are reluctant to leave the family home? Similar to Cassie, today's youth are starting from a negative position. Financial life planning for those born after 1985 will be dramatically different than it has been for earlier generations.

Sample 1 shows you a simplified chart of the differences between the Boomers and Generation Y.

SAMPLE 1
Differences between the Baby Boomers and Generation Y

Age	Cassie's Parents	Cassie
Born	Baby boomer: 1945 to 1964	Generation Y: 1985 to 1995
Age 18	Complete high school; select few go to college or university	Complete high school; apply for college or university
Age 19	Enter workforce	Enter university with easy access to student loans
Age 21	Traditional wedding	Still in university
Ages 22 to 25	Purchase first home in the suburbs	Complete university with substantial debt
NET WORTH Age 25	Adjusted for inflation +$14,000 (approximately)	−$20,000.00

My question to you is: How can you take advantage of your unique situation and give yourself a quick start to the next decade? If you follow the steps outlined in the subsequent chapters, you will be off to a good start.

CHAPTER TWO

Give Your Parents the "Money Talk"

* Read this if you are a student and you want to know how much help you can expect from your parents.

* Read this if you have recently graduated and you want to live at home while looking for a job and/or starting your career.

Regardless of whether you are living in the family home or have already moved to a place on your own, I strongly recommend you have the "money talk" with your parents. Fashions and social mores may have changed, but what has not changed is parents' love for their children and their desire to see them off to a good start as they begin life's journey.

All parents have expectations for their children. Sometimes these expectations are heard loud and clear. At other times it seems like expectations are secret until one of you experiences disappointment with the other. It is best to have an open dialogue with your parents about the expectations you have of each other. During this dialogue you may find that your expectations of each other are similar or you may discover that your ideas do *not* coincide. That said, this is important information for each of you to know in advance.

The purpose of this conversation is to gain a clear understanding of what you can and should expect from your parents. While it is your parents' responsibility to raise children to become self-sufficient adults, this does *not* mean giving in to your every wish. Thus, you must recognize your parents also need to be planning for their own retirement — unless of course you would prefer to support them in their old age! Be respectful and let your parents know how grateful you are to them for all the support they have given and are willing to provide you.

If you and your parents are able to have an open dialogue on these topics, I believe all of you will gain greater insight into the values which are important to each of you. What values do you share? In which ways are you different? You will also have a good idea of the amount of financial support you can expect while you're a student and after graduation. Knowing what to expect from your parents will help you develop a strategy for meeting your educational and career goals. The rest will be up to you.

1. Topics to Discuss with Your Parents

The following topics are intended to serve as a guide. You may wish to add some of your own. Begin with the questions you feel most comfortable asking. Similar to Cassie's example in Chapter 1, you may wish to begin by asking your parents about their own early years and the values they believe led to their success.

1.1 Values

Each family is guided by the values in which they believe. You might call it the moral compass for what is right and wrong, good and evil, and smart or foolish. Families may not often speak of their values, yet family values drive decision making. A lively discussion can be had by talking to your parents about your family's values. A greater understanding of family values will assist you in developing your own personal value system. The following are some samples to begin your discussion:

- **Ethical values:** Honesty, justice, trust, and fairness

- **Personal values:** Modesty, gratitude, loyalty and faithfulness, diligence, and perseverance

- **Relationships:** The importance of family, friends, and colleagues at work, church, and community

- **Emotional values:** Compassion, kindness, and generosity

- **Health:** Good health, physical fitness, relaxation, regular medical and dental care, protecting one's good health, longevity, and care of the ill or disabled

1.2 Education

Many parents, given the financial means, are prepared to assist their children in the quest for higher education. Parental values and financial abilities may differ. Some parents are prepared to pay for their child's education while others believe their children will benefit by contributing to the cost; and some are ill-prepared to assist their children in any capacity.

Asking the following questions of your parents will provide you with important information as you choose your educational path:

- Is it important to you that I achieve a college diploma? University degree? Beyond? Why?

- Do you have the resources to help pay for my education?

- Can I expect your support while I am completing my post-secondary education? To what extent?

- If you can help me financially, how much can you contribute?

- Can I live at home while going to school or would it be better if I lived on campus?

- Will I have access to transportation (e.g., a vehicle or help with paying for a bus pass)?

- Am I expected to pay my own way by using scholarships, applying for student loans, and/or getting part-time work?

1.3 Returning to the family home after graduation

What can you expect of your parents once you have graduated, assuming you wish to live in the family home until you are employed? Is it necessary for me to mention that you are now an adult and as such you cannot expect a free ride? For example, many parents are agreeable to adult children living with them while in school or while looking for a job. These same parents may not look kindly upon children planning to live at home while lazing around all day playing video games and entertaining friends. For many parents this would, rightfully, be the deal breaker.

Maintaining a home costs your parents money. What are the monthly expenses for maintaining the family home? Think about the cost of a mortgage, utilities, food, and the use of a car. Discuss this with your parents; you may be surprised at their answers. Now consider how much you can afford to contribute as your fair portion. Be grateful for your parents' support and remember, it is your parents' home, and as an adult, you are a guest. As such, you should be prepared to contribute something and abide by your parents' values.

Before moving back in with your parents it is a good idea to ask them the following questions:

- How long am I welcome in the family home after graduation (e.g., one year, two years, longer)?

- What can I do to contribute to the household while living in the family home (e.g., chores, purchase groceries, pay bills)?

- How much rent can I afford to pay? How much rent do you want me to pay?

- Do you plan to assist me when I move out of the house? *The ability and willingness to help varies among parents. Some are prepared to help financially (e.g., a contribution to the security deposit for the new apartment), while others will give their children home-cooked meals, old furniture, and anything else to see them off to a good start.*

- What are the house rules while I am living with you? *The house rules will more than likely be different than when you were a teenager and in high school. New rules for privacy, lifestyles, and housekeeping may be implemented.*

Your parents may be so happy to see you launched into the big, wide world they will give you kitchen items, furniture, TVs, and computers that have been collecting dust in the basement. Accept all gifts gratefully, even if you end up re-gifting the items later on. Consider the money saved by not having to purchase everything at once.

Let's reflect on Cassie's situation again. Cassie asks the questions above and is very surprised by what she learns. She discovers that her parents have very definite ideas about her future, some of which they have been planning for many years.

Since her parents did not have the luxury to complete university, having Cassie complete university was very important to Cano and Francesca. They are very proud of her accomplishment.

Francesca and Cano are happy to have Cassie stay in the family home while she searches for a full-time position. Cassie tells them it may take her up to six months to secure a full-time job.

Cassie asks herself, "What if after three months of searching for my dream job I am unable to secure a position?" After three months of looking she is prepared to accept an entry level position with a major industry employer, just to get in the door. Not only are her parents happy to help, they worry about her student debt and realize Cassie will need to save for her first and last month's rent. She will also need an emergency fund. Cassie and her parents agree that she is welcome in the family home for up to a year after she is employed, on the condition that she uses this time to reduce her debt and start a savings program. Cassie will be expected to help with the household chores and do the yard work while she is in their home.

Cassie is feeling a lot better about her future. She is very much aware of her parents' love and grateful for their support. With her parents' help she will have a solid start to becoming self-reliant.

CHAPTER THREE

Steps for Students

* Read this if you are a student.

* Read this if you want to know how to get on the best path to a solid well-paying career.

* Read this if you wonder about the value of part-time work and volunteerism while a student.

Graduate students with no prior work or volunteer experience are at a distinct disadvantage. Prospective employers rely on the referrals of past employers, even if the jobs are not related. Naturally, those with past work experience, even in menial jobs, will find it easier to convince a potential employer of their value.

Embrace volunteer and part-time work as part of your informal education, for here is where you will learn about life, work, and money before you are expected to pay your own way.

1. Course Selection Leading to Success

Careful selection of your educational program is required to make the best use of your student years. The decisions you make now will determine, to a great extent, your future career path and financial well-being.

If your education will be funded with student loans, it is imperative you are able to repay this debt in a reasonable amount of time after you graduate. Ask yourself the following questions:

- How much of my educational costs will be funded by debt?

- Will I be able to repay this debt once I graduate?

Unless you were fortunate enough to be born into a family of wealth, and your parents are agreeable to supporting your academic aspirations without limit, serious thought must be given to what the payoff will be.

You will want to take courses that interest you and for which you have a natural talent. When choosing between two areas of study, why not take the path with the highest reward-to-cost ratio?

In other words, do the math: How much is your education going to cost, relative to the income potential? For example, dental hygienist versus dentist: The typical dental hygienist will earn $40,000 to $70,000. A dentist may make five times as much. Consideration must be given to the higher level of academic achievement required, the number of years before becoming licensed to practice, and the amount of debt upon graduation. Both of these choices are a solid career choice.

Do not ignore college and trade school offerings. Some of these offer solid career options with good earning potential. If you think that skilled trades are limited to carpenter, electrician, plumber, or welder, think again. A quick web search for skilled trades turned up an alphabet soup of viable options, including the following career options: accounts payroll administrator, dental chair-side assistant, legal assistant, massage therapist, pharmacy assistant, and video game designer.

Many trade programs run from one to four years, including time spent as an apprentice. Students who are in an apprentice program earn a modest living while they train for their future profession. Sometimes employers sponsor the students by paying for books and tuition. This is a good opportunity to show a potential future employer your skills and suitability for full-time employment.

Avoid the "ugly dance." The ugly dancer does not have a clear picture of where he or she is going. Without an end goal in mind, he or she takes two steps forward, changes direction, heads four steps back, does a 180-degree twirl, and ends up facing the opposite direction. The ugly dancer lacks a clear plan for success. These are the students you may have read about, who graduate with a major in "basket weaving" and $100,000 in student loans. Not realizing the job prospects and pay scale for basket weaving means a lifetime of paying student debt on a barista's paycheck. It is important to know that student loans in both the United States and Canada are not necessarily forgiven if you declare bankruptcy.[1] Student debt could be with you for a very long time.

The smartest students are strategic. They take a strategic approach to reach desired career goals. In contrast to the ugly dance students, the strategic type will spend considerable time researching not only his or her course options but also the career paths available after graduation, the expected pay scales, and potential employers. He or she conducts research online, talks to guidance counselors, consults older friends already in the workforce, and seeks professionals in his or her fields of interest. The strategic type finds the organizations doing the type of work he or she is interested in. He or she contacts these organizations, asking to speak to someone who can provide advice on what he or she should be doing *now* so he or she is ready to enter the workforce upon graduation. Most people like to be helpful, so contacting people in the industry is a surprisingly useful way to get acquainted with a potential future employer.

The strategic approach is to define the desired career goals and develop a strategy for success. The following are some of the things a strategic student would consider.

- **Evaluate the skill set and academic abilities:** Most students choose courses based on their skill sets and academic ability, but ask yourself, "Do I have the discipline to complete the program I am considering?" and "Will I persevere when times get tough?"

- **Understand how much time and money will be required:** Are you prepared? How many years will be devoted to pursuing your degree? How much will it cost? Where will the funds come from?

- **Use the principal of Other People's Money (OPM):** Take the time to research and apply for all available scholarships and bursaries. There is money out there, it just takes a little effort to find it. Money from scholarships and bursaries means less debt after graduation.

---

[1] Canadian Student Loan Bankruptcy Blog, "Canada Student Loan Bankruptcy Legislation," www.student-loan-bankruptcy.ca, (2011), accessed June 2011.

- **Estimate the level of debt at graduation:** The strategic student attempts to minimize the total amount of debt. He or she is self-reliant, keeping debt under control with part-time work. This type of student plans in advance and has a good idea how much debt will be required to complete the desired program. He or she formulates a repayment plan.

- **Ease of entry into the workforce:** Though it is impossible to fully know the market in advance, this student has considered the market for his or her new skills. This person asks, "If employers are hiring graduates, what are the expected pay scales and future career opportunities?

- **Know the payoff relative to cost of education:** This is the big one. Does the ratio of total cost compared to projections of future income make this a wise choice? Education is expensive and is becoming more so every year. It is one area of our economy in which costs are increasing faster than the rate of inflation.

If you are unsure of your unique ability or have difficulty describing your most valuable skill set, you may wish to take the online Kolbe Index A test.[2] Discover your natural unique ability and mode of operating. I highly recommend this short quiz of 36 questions (there is a fee) and have personally used it for more than a decade to better understand my family, employees, and potential employees' instinctive problem-solving methods. The results will provide you with insight into your own unique strengths as well as valuable information which you can use when trying to choose the educational program to match your unique mode of operating. The Kolbe A Index test results provide examples of professions and occupations which suit your unique ability.

You will find the information in this chapter easier to apply after you read Chapter 6, "Set Goals"; and Chapter 7, "Create a Budget." Once you have read these chapters and completed the worksheets, you will have a clear picture of where you are today and what needs to be done to reach your education goals.

2. Part-Time Work and the Student

The local newspaper is delivered to my home each and every week as faithfully as the daily mail. Every week a young boy carefully places

---

[2] Kolbe, "Kolbe A Index," www.kolbe.com, (2008), accessed June 2011.

the paper between the front door and the screen. The first week of each month he arrives just before dinner, when he knows his customers will be home, to collect for the preceding month. His smile lights up the doorway, and his sincere thank-you warms my heart. I have my eye out for this future young man. In him, I see the businessman of tomorrow, who will attract record results for his employer with his attention to detail and the level of service he provides. He is eight years old!

There is no such thing as a "menial" job. Every job experience you have will build skills for your future success. Set the stage for future career success with part-time work while in high school or university. The actual work can vary. It does not matter if you stack shelves at the local grocery store, flip burgers, wash dishes, move refrigerators, paint homes, or cut lawns. Each and every one of these jobs will help you build invaluable skills that you will use in future workplaces.

There are many advantages to working while still a student, the most immediate of which is cash to pay for your hobbies, and cover the cost of books, transportation, and out-of-pocket expenses.

Other advantages include:

- Independence and cash of your own to provide you with the freedom to make financial decisions of your own choosing.

- Reducing the amount of student loans required to complete your education.

- Increased confidence. Even working at low-paying jobs will provide you with the opportunity to better understand your unique skills and the value of your contribution to the workplace.

- Learning the value of teamwork.

- Becoming familiar with workplace demands and employer expectations.

- Learning about a career *before* committing to it.

- Acquiring skills to help sell yourself to a prospective employer. Practice your future job hunting and interviewing skills early and often by applying for part-time work while still a student. Doing so means you will be better prepared for an important career interview. You will understand what to expect and how to conduct yourself in an interview.

- Work experience gained while a student allows you to fill your résumé with practical real life experiences and a source of character references.

The real advantage of part-time work while you are a student has nothing to do with the money you are paid, but rather the knowledge gained; the knowledge that you are capable of handling responsibility, you can be trusted, and you are accountable for your actions. Part-time jobs build character and confidence, which will be priceless when it comes to landing your dream job.

You may find the part-time work you do as a student becomes the base for your future career direction. Or, you may decide a career you were interested in is not right for you. The friends and contacts made during these years will provide a valuable resource in the future as you move to full-time employment.

3. Volunteer Work

Do not overlook volunteerism. Volunteer work and responsibilities on a résumé add credibility and provide a prospective employer with a glimpse into your character.

How would *you* like to add the following credential to your résumé: "The Humanitarian," the Annual Award to College Hockey's Finest Citizen?[3] Jason Cupp[4] was nominated and won this award in 2001 for his tireless work to assist underprivileged children with the program he developed called "Scoring for Kids," which introduces children to ice hockey. Cupp has always been an active volunteer, supporting multiple sclerosis and the Children's Miracle Network while continuing to coach hockey and teach guitar in his spare time.

Much of Cupp's efforts have been devoted to the Scoring for Kids program. The program, which was his brainchild, is designed to promote cultural diversity in youth hockey and to give disadvantaged children exposure to ice sports. Through his efforts, he has solicited more than $10,000 from individual foundations and corporations to help fund the Scoring for Kids program.

---

[3] Hockey Humanitarian, "Hockey Humanitarian Award," www.hockeyhumanitarian.org, (2011), accessed June 2011.

[4] Hockey Humanitarian, "Jason Cupp 2001 Recipient," www.hockeyhumanitarian.org/page/show/292843-jason-cupp-2001-recipient, (2001), accessed June 2011.

This fine young man is a close family friend. In the years since graduating, Cupp has always been able to secure a position of choice in what can only be described as a "tight" labor market. Cupp is now a teacher in Ontario, Canada. It is my understanding that Ontario is graduating many more teachers per year than there are available positions, yet Cupp has never been without a job.

Cupp told me the recognition he received for his volunteer work continues to be the highlight of his résumé.

An unexpected benefit was the interview process he had to undergo before being awarded the Humanitarian of the Year Award. This prepared him for the interview process he would encounter when applying for work. He was also required to make a speech to an audience of several hundred people; Cupp recognized all of these as opportunities to grow beyond his comfort zone. Doing so demonstrated his character — his willingness to do what was important, rather than what he liked.

CHAPTER FOUR

From School to Workplace

* Read this section if you are a new graduate about to enter the workforce.

* Read this section if you are considering career options and trying to choose the best overall offer.

There are numerous books, guides, and websites dedicated to helping you write a résumé, attend interviews, and land a job. This brief chapter is not designed to replace those resources. Rather, as an employer, I am sharing my personal experiences and point of view.

1. What Employers Want from You

If you recently graduated and are now looking for a full-time career, this may come as a huge shock to you: Employers do not care about your Grade Point Average (GPA)!

I know you just spent the last several years trying to impress your school, teachers, and parents with your superior intelligence. You busted your buns, spent countless nights in the library slumped over unreadable text to add half a point to your overall grade. Do not be surprised when your college friend who barely graduated calls to tell you he landed the dream job you coveted all through university.

You may have emailed your fine résumé clearly outlining your grades and demonstrating your superior intellect. What happened? Did your résumé get misplaced?

The truth is, the position went to the applicant who was best able to communicate his or her unique ability to add value to the firm, and demonstrated his or her passion with persistence and ingenuity. Not only did this applicant use the Internet, he or she most likely resorted to old-fashioned cold calling and networking. The applicant may have joined professional organizations and done volunteer work in his or her chosen field to provide the best possible advantage. Use the principle of relationship leverage and get in touch with the people you know who have influence, and ask them for their help. Most people like to be thought of as helpful, so make a clear statement of what you are looking for and then request their help.

Employers do not hire the applicant with the highest grades. They are looking for the person who will bring the most value to their company. Value can be defined by the service you provide — the "service" category is dominated by government or quasi-government positions such as teaching and law enforcement. Businesses define value primarily by the following two criteria: How much money you can make for the company (i.e., sales and marketing positions fall into his category) and how much money you can save the company (i.e., accounting and finance are positions that help corporations save money).

Potential employers want to know if you can do the following:

- Provide a résumé that demonstrates your contribution to past employers and your community.

- Communicate your value and worth, deliver a valued service, and increase sales or cost savings.

- Communicate your employer's value and worth to prospective clients.

- Save money for the company.

- Increase sales and/or revenue.

- Meet important deadlines even if it means you arrive early and leave late.

If you are unsure of your unique ability or have difficulty describing your most valuable skill set, you may wish to take the online Kolbe Index A test mentioned in Chapter 3. The results will provide you with insight into your own unique strengths as well as valuable information on how to describe your unique skills to a potential employer.

Consider how you can best contribute to a company and then tell prospective employers, loud and clear, with a well-written résumé. The best way to do this is to research and tailor your résumé and cover letter to appeal to your potential employers and the industry in which you want to work. Researching your potential employers will allow you to demonstrate you know who they are and have a passion for the work they do.

When you tailor your résumé, remember there may be merit in telling Greenpeace about your "green" beliefs, but if you tell that to an oil company, be prepared to back it up with how this can help the oil industry and your prospective employer improve its public image and give it a competitive advantage.

Many community service groups offer professional résumé-writing programs. Take advantage of the help available in your community.

2. Decide What You Want from the Employer

If you are lucky, you may be offered two positions (or more) and have to choose between them. How do you make the best choice? You will need to consider the following:

- How much you will be paid.

- How secure the position is (e.g., permanent, contract, or temporary).

- How your income will change over time. How often are employees evaluated and how quickly are new hires promoted?

- What the opportunities for advancement include. For example, a small employer may offer few chances for advancement whereas a large employer may have a history of promoting internally from the mail room to the executive suite.

- What type of benefits are offered and when they begin (e.g., health, dental, and life and disability insurance).

Consider the locational advantage as well. A locational advantage exists where a position offers the same pay scale across the country. Many social service or government positions offer similar pay scales, regardless of location. Teachers, nurses, and law enforcement officers fall into this category; even your mail delivery person. When applying for these positions, you may want to consider applying in smaller cities and towns where the cost of housing is lower. If you consider that the cost of living in a large city can be thousands of dollars more each and every year, the same professional living in a smaller town has a distinct and measurable locational advantage; the professional living in a small town will have more cash in his or her pocket. This person is then in a better position to pay down student loans; buy a vehicle or big screen TV; purchase a home; or simply enjoy a better lifestyle. Consider what additional cost will be incurred or saved by accepting a position.

When making your decision to accept a position, consider the size of employer. Small firms, including family-run companies, may be more nimble and offer more opportunities for making your personal mark but lack internal growth opportunities and offer fewer benefits. Large employers will be more rigid, but they offer opportunities for advancement and generally have generous insurance plans including health and dental, and income replacement. They may also offer pension plans. Positions with government bodies are generally very rigid, but they tend to provide the greatest level of job security and generous benefit packages including health and dental and income insurance as well as pension plans. So how do you know which pay package offers the highest compensation? The following example will help you make a decision:

- Job A offers a starting salary of $54,500 with no benefits.

- Job B offers a starting salary of $45,000. Your benefits include savings to a retirement plan equal to 10 percent of your salary paid by your employer, as well as health and dental benefits (it is safe to assume the employer's cost is 6 percent of salary). In addition, Job B offers sick pay in the event you have an accident or become too ill to work. You check the cost of purchasing a long-term disability insurance plan and discover the annual premiums would cost $2,500 if you had to purchase it on your own.

Let's compare the two jobs in Sample 2.

SAMPLE 2
Comparing a Job with Benefits versus a Job without Benefits

	Job A	Job B
Salary	$54,500	$45,000
Retirement savings		4,500
Health and dental		2,700
Long-term disability		2,500
Total compensation	**$54,500**	**$54,700**

Are you surprised? The total compensation package of Job B is higher than Job A. Do not underestimate the value of a benefits package. Be prepared to ask questions about benefit programs. Responsible employers are eager to offer competitive benefits. The benefits form an important part of your compensation, so consider their value before accepting competing positions.

Now consider the impact of your employer making a 10 percent contribution to your retirement plan over a 25-year period. Assuming your income rises with inflation at a rate of 3 percent and the investments earn 7 percent annually, the value of your employer-paid nest egg would be approximately $400,000! Keep this in mind, think about your own personality, and ask yourself: "Would I save this on my own?"

When choosing to leave a current employer for a new position, remember to add the value of your existing benefits to your current pay scale. Generally I do not advise my clients to make a switch unless the new employer's offer is at least 20 percent higher. If the new position is with a small firm or a start-up without benefits, consider how much you will have to pay out of your pocket to duplicate your existing benefits. Now subtract this amount from the employer's offer to see the true value of the compensation. The value of a benefits package can easily exceed 25 percent of the salary.

CHAPTER FIVE

From Your Parents' Basement to Your First Apartment

* Read this if you are planning to leave the family nest in the next 6 to 36 months, and you are looking forward to being independent and having a place of your own.

* Read this if you want to have a solid financial foundation as you embark on your own.

If you put your time and money to good use while living at home with your parents, you will begin life as a self-sufficient adult. Living at home offers you the time to increase your savings for your first apartment and pay down a large portion of student debt. Whether your income is from part-time work or your first full-time position, you will never have more disposable income than while living in the family home. This provides the perfect opportunity to save for your move to financial self-reliance.

If you are planning to move back into the family home, and you are working, offer to pay your parents a portion of your income toward the household operating costs. Paying your way is the first step to fiscal responsibility, and it will help you feel better about yourself. Tell your parents how long you expect to stay in the family home. Set a time limit for how long you will stay, and begin now to plan the steps you need to take to leave the family home for a place of your own.

1. Begin with a Savings Plan

Before you bolt out the door, you need to consider how much money you will need to get started. For example, landlords generally require a deposit equal to one or two months' rent.

Prudent financial wisdom recommends that you have an emergency fund equal to three to six months' income. An emergency fund will help you to meet unexpected future costs such as the loss of a job, or an expensive vehicle repair. You will also likely need a few dollars to purchase furniture and other items for your new home.

While you are still living in the family home, create a simple savings plan, which may look similar to this:

- 30 percent of your (after tax) income to your apartment fund and emergency fund.

- 30 percent toward your debt (student loans plus credit cards).

- 40 percent (the remainder) for your transportation, cell phone, Internet, clothing, entertainment, vacations, etc.

Now is the time to consider your starting point. What is the value of your assets? How much do you owe? The difference between these two numbers is your *net worth*.

How much money do you earn each month? What are your fixed monthly expenses? What is remaining? A *cash flow statement* can be used to show this information and will indicate if there is a surplus or a shortfall.

All of these topics will be explored in greater detail in Chapter 7, "Create a Budget"; and Chapter 8, "Calculate Your Net Worth." After reading these chapters, you will be able to create a cash flow statement and a net worth statement of your own by using the templates provided.

Lets' go back to Cassie and see how she is doing after graduation. Cassie is hired as an editor's assistant which pays $3,000 a month after taxes. Cassie needs to pay for her cell phone, transportation, and personal expenses such as clothing, gym membership, and dining out. She has promised to pay her parents $200 a month to help with the household operating costs. She has $950 in savings, but she owes $20,000 in student loans.

Cassie is determined to have a place of her own by this time next year, but before she moves, she wants to reduce her debt. She develops the following savings plan:

- Her student loan is due over a ten-year period with payments of $220 a month. She is anxious to quickly pay this loan so she tops up each payment by $400 a month for a total of $620.

- Cassie estimates her rent will be approximately $900 a month so she will need $1,800 to sign a lease. She begins a savings plan and adds $150 a month.

- In addition, Cassie needs an emergency fund. She saves $800 a month. One year from today she will have $9,600 in savings — enough to withstand an emergency.

While Cassie's net worth statement a year later is still a negative number, she has made great progress and is only a few months away from having a positive net worth, and a few years away from clearing her student loan completely. One reason Cassie may choose to keep paying her student loan on a regular schedule, rather than pay it off in full, is the low interest rates available for this kind of debt. This will provide Cassie some flexibility when making other purchases on credit cards where the rate of interest charged is much higher. Cassie uses the remainder of $270 per month to buy clothing and furniture, and for entertainment, travel, and hobbies. See Samples 3 and 4 for Cassie's Cash Flow Statement and Cassie's Net Worth.

SAMPLE 3
Cassie's Cash Flow Statement

	Monthly	After 1 Year
Cash Inflows		
Employment income after tax and deductions	$3,000	$36,000
Cash Outflows/Lifestyle Expenses		
Cell phone	$60	$720
Personal expenses	300	3,600
Transportation	600	7,200
Monthly payment to parents	200	2,400
Student loan (10 years)	220	2,640
Total Expenses	**$1,380**	**$16,560**
Savings		
Apartment fund	$150	$1,800
Emergency fund	800	9,600
Loan top-up	400	4,800
Total Savings	**$1,350**	**$16,200**
Remainder	**$270**	**$3,240**

SAMPLE 4
Cassie's Net Worth

	Now	12 Months Later
Savings		
Cash	$950	$600
Emergency fund		9,600
Subtotal	**$950**	**$10,200**
Liabilities		
Student loan	$20,000	$13,500
Total Net Worth	**−$19,050**	**−$3,300**

2. Selecting an Apartment

Finally: School is finished, you have a job, some money saved, and you are ready for your first apartment. Now what?

The first step is to create a budget. Be careful to include all of your existing commitments such as transportation costs, cell phone, loan payments, and so on. If you have a vehicle, include the cost of insurance, gas, and regular maintenance. (See Chapter 7 for more information about creating a budget.)

Start with your budget in mind. A good rule of thumb is that your rent should not exceed 30 percent of your after-tax income. You may want to consider shared accommodation just to be closer to your job and to reduce your rent. Remember the less you spend on rent, the more money you have left over for other things.

Consider transportation between your apartment, work, and family and friends. Your apartment should be easily accessible to the places you frequent the most. How long will it take you to get to work or to travel to visit friends and family?

Where you live will have a great bearing on the cost. Large cities can have very high rents, forcing you to spend more, live in a less desirable neighborhood, or live on the outskirts of the city. If you live on the outskirts of the city, that could mean an increase in gas mileage if your job is in the city center. If you don't have a vehicle, you will need to consider whether or not the transportation (e.g., bus, subway) will be adequate. Will it cost more for a bus pass the further away you live from the city center? Money isn't the only cost when it comes to transportation; consider the amount of time you will spend commuting.

If you have a budget, and you have a good idea of the area in which you would like to live, start looking at some options within your budget. The more places you see, the better you will get at judging what you like and what works for you. Go and inspect at least ten apartments in different buildings. Take your time. If you do not find what you are looking for, keep looking. It is a good idea to take a day or two to consider your choices before signing a lease. Once you have identified an apartment you like, ask for a copy of the lease, take it home with you, and read it. Understand what you are signing, and if you are not sure, use a highlighter and ask your potential landlord for an explanation of highlighted sections.

Make sure you ask what utilities are included in the rent (e.g., electricity, gas, parking, cable, Internet). If utilities aren't included, you will need to determine how much the additional costs will be. Add these extra costs to the rental amount. Make sure you are still within your budget.

If you are responsible for paying for your own utilities, call the providers and ask about security deposits. Frequently, providers of utilities will require you to pay a security deposit before they give you an account. Each of these may be several hundreds of dollars. Note that payment is required *before* service is connected. Before saying yes to an apartment where you are responsible for your utilities, it is a good idea to ask the utility providers for a letter of preapproval.

You should do a walk-through with the landlord. If there is any damage to the place, it should be noted by both the landlord and you — preferably in an inspection report (meaning written down) and signed by both you and the landlord at the end of the walk-through. It may also be a good idea to take pictures of any damages to the rental property before you move in, so when you move out, you can prove you did not contribute to the previously documented damages (this should also be done with the landlord present). Ask the landlord if, prior to you moving in, the apartment will be painted, carpets cleaned, and appliances cleaned and inspected. Some landlords do all of the preceding, some do none. You may be able to negotiate some or all of these.

Sometimes it is possible to negotiate the rent. Do not be shy; if you ask politely and you clearly state your other options, you may find you are able to reduce the rent from the original asking price. This is where your research pays off because you now know what the comparable choices are. Early in the conversation, let your landlord know you are on a budget. Then try this question, "Is this your best price for this apartment? I am comparing several, and it would help me to make a decision if I know your best price."

When you have found the place you want, you will be asked to sign a lease. Most leases have a one-year term. This can usually be renewed annually. Note that rents do increase over time. As you sign the lease your landlord will request a two-month deposit. Half will be applied to your first month's rent. The balance will be held as either the last month's rent or a security deposit. This will be returned at the end of the lease after the landlord has inspected the property to ensure there are no damages. Assuming you completed an inspection report with your landlord prior to signing a lease, you can then verify that the condition of the apartment did not suffer while you were a tenant.

Congratulations! You are now a fully self-reliant adult. You have completed a strategic methodology to achieving your educational, career, and first apartment goals. Take a few minutes and thank those who helped you through your student days. Thank your parents for their love and support as you start your new life in your new home. Better yet, invite them over for a nice dinner!

CHAPTER SIX

Set Goals

* Read this if you have great plans for your future and want to give yourself the best possible odds.

* Read this if you have some ideas for your future, but are unsure how to prioritize what is most important.

* Don't read this if you are a parent hoping to map out a life plan for your child. The only one who can do this exercise is the one who will live it.

In this chapter you will learn to set goals. These goals will provide the groundwork for the direction your life will take in the next two, five, and ten years. Commit to your new behaviors and strategies and be surprised by what you will accomplish.

Your twenties is the decade when you begin to make choices on your own and for yourself — the most important person to please is *you*. Up until now, your parents, teachers, and coaches may have made decisions for you; and although they are still there to help and guide you, more and more frequently the form of that help will be to allow you to make wise choices on your own. The decisions you make now will have a great impact on your future happiness and success. It is worth taking the time to think about what *you* want out of life and the steps you are prepared to take to achieve your goals. Setting goals is the first step in your financial life plan.

1. Set Your Goals

With a little thought, you will be able to make wise choices most of the time. Of course, some decisions may not turn out exactly as planned, but think of these as learning experiences. Your twenties set the stage for the rest of your life. These are the years when you will build the inner confidence that comes to those in their thirties. In my experience, confidence and happiness are inseparable. Confidence earned by making wise choices leads to your personal happiness.

By doing the exercises in this chapter you will quickly realize some of your goals are achievable within the next year or two, while others may take five or more years to accomplish. It is helpful to sort your goals by the amount of time it will take to achieve each goal. Take a look at Sample 5.

SAMPLE 5
Setting Goals

Goal	Time to Complete	Example
Short-term goals	2 years or less	Planning and saving for a holiday
Mid-term goals	2 to 7 years	Saving for a home
Long-term goals	7 years or more	Retirement

When saving money for your goals it is a good idea to set up savings accounts for each goal. Use automatic deposits from your bank account to your savings accounts to ensure money is moved systematically. That way you will not be tempted to take money from your "home purchase" account to pay for a short-term "holiday" goal.

1.1 Step 1: Visualization

Visualization techniques are frequently used by professionals in many fields — such as actors, athletes, investment advisors, and real estate agents — to improve their performance. Visualization allows these successful professionals to achieve the results they desire by imagining them first.

The basic premise of visualization is to imagine what you want and then use that image to create your desired reality. By doing the visualization exercises, you will gain a better understanding of what is important to you. If you have never done visualization before, these exercises may challenge you. Visualizing your goals is an important part of achieving them. No one can see you, so go ahead and give it a try.

Exercise 1, Visualization, is designed specifically to help you think about and set goals for what is most important to you. Begin with imagining your ideal life; at this stage, there is no need to be specific. Simply roll with whatever comes to your mind.

Exercise 1 is where you will answer the power question; for example, "If you and I were to meet again in two, five, and ten years from today, reflecting on your progress over that time, what would you have to accomplish for you to feel good about yourself?" This question challenges you to imagine yourself in the future looking back on today. This one question can change your life. Answer it and you will be able to identify the specific goals you need to achieve in the next two, five, and ten years to feel good about yourself and your progress.

You will need to find a calming place to think about and work through the exercise. Find a quiet spot where you will not be disturbed. There should be no outside distractions, no music, no TV, and no computer. Most important, turn off your cell phone!

Now it is time to relax and think about your goals. It is a good idea to do these exercises on a regular basis. When you have achieved one goal on your list, you may want to do the visualization exercises again, updating your goal matrix.

The final three questions in Part 2 of Exercise 1 can be asked in several areas of your life. It might relate to your education, your career, or even your love life. Where do you see yourself in two, five, and ten years? While answering this question you will begin to focus on your specific goals for the next decade. If a decade is too long for you to imagine, focus on the next two to five years. Write down your specific goals on a slip of paper. Place it in your wallet. I will tell you why soon!

This simple exercise of imagining yourself in the future, answering the power question, and handwriting your goals will help you to commit your goals to memory. Take the additional step of selecting photos to represent the goals you visualized. Later you will attach a list of your goals and photos to Exercise 2. Selecting the photos of what you want to achieve and posting them in a prominent place will remind you of what you are going to achieve. Want to increase your odds? Tell someone close to you about your future goals. Remember the more senses you engage, the more likely you are to achieve your goals.

To confirm how well this exercise works, open your wallet one year from now, take out your handwritten copy and read it. I promise you, you will be amazed at how much progress you have made toward your two-, five-, and ten-year goals.

EXERCISE 1
Visualization

Part 1: Visualization

This exercise may take 15 to 30 minutes to complete.

In a quiet and comfortable spot, begin by taking few deep breaths. Close your eyes. Imagine a clear day and a big blue sky. Try to involve as many of your senses as possible. Now imagine your ideal future.

The following suggestions and questions may help you to begin:

- You are in your favorite place. This could be an old favorite or some place you have only imagined being.
- What does it feel like?
- What are you doing?
- Are you participating in your favorite sport?
- Are you working at a job you love?
- Are you alone?
- Is someone with you?

Include as much detail as possible. For example, you are thinking about your dream car, what is the make, color, and year? Where are you driving? How do you feel in it?

Topics to review during your visualization exercise should include:

- How you feel, how confident, and how happy you are.
- Feel the respect of your peers, friends, and family.
- Your dream career and the adrenaline rush you get from doing what you love.
- How much money you are making.
- What is your lifestyle?
- Do you live in a vibrant big city or small town full of old friends?

Once you are done, write the images from this exercise on a slip of paper. Include as much detail as possible. Place a copy in your wallet.

Part 2: You in the Future

The power question: If you and I were to meet again two, five, and ten years from today, reflecting on your progress over that time, what would you have to accomplish for you to feel good about yourself? This question challenges you to imagine yourself in the future looking back on today.

Year 2

What have you accomplished?

_____

Do you feel good about yourself?

_____

What could you have done better?

_____

Year 5

What have you accomplished?

_____

Do you feel good about yourself?

_____

What could you have done better?

_____

Year 10

What have you accomplished?

_____

Do you feel good about yourself?

_____

What could you have done better?

_____

1.2 Step 2: Goals, Position, and Strategy (GPS)

The earlier you begin to define what you want out of life the faster you will get there. Consider this the Goals, Position, and Strategy (GPS) for your life.

Plug in your destination and watch the road to your goals unfold. Using a GPS, you can see your current location plus the next few blocks; or you can set the program to see the entire route to your final destination. You can plan stops along the way, or go directly to your destination. Like a GPS for traveling in a car, planning your life is no different. You can only arrive at your destination if you know in advance where you want to go. Otherwise, you end up driving around aimlessly looking for something but not sure how to get there.

You have completed Exercise 1 and you have written down your goals, selected photos that represent your goals, and told a friend. Now you are ready to complete Exercise 2. Use Exercise 2 as a guide to help you think about the areas of your life to include. Feel free to add topics, or substitute the ones listed for goals you have identified for yourself. The exercise is set up for you to record your goals, evaluate your current position, and create a strategy for success.

Once you have identified your goals, you will want to prioritize them. Place the most important ones at the top of your list. After all, this is *your* life and only you can know what is important to *you*. Write down your goals in the "Goals" column.

The next step is to take stock of your current position. Where are you today? Write this in the "Position Today" column.

The final step is to think about your success strategy; what it will take to achieve your goals and how much time is required to complete each goal? Are you prepared to give up one goal in order to achieve a larger goal? For each goal, what steps will you have to take to accomplish your desired result? Record your answers under the "Success Strategy" column.

Add your goals, current position, and your success strategies to Exercise 2. Just like a GPS in your vehicle that tells you the distance to your destination and provides you with clear directions, completion of this exercise will provide a record of the important goals in your life and directions to your destination. Now commit to your plan of action! Review your completed Exercise 2 often to see if you are on target or not.

EXERCISE 2
Goals, Position, and Strategy (GPS)

Areas to Consider	Goals What do you want most?	Position Today What is your current position?	Success Strategy What steps do you need to take for success?
Education			
Career			
Savings			
Debt repayment			
First apartment			
Marriage			
First home purchase			
Business of your own			
Major purchase (e.g., vehicle, holiday)			
Other			

1.3 Step 3: Dangers, Opportunities, and Strengths (DOS)

The DOS analysis is a tool to help you consider the inherent *dangers* of the goals and strategies you are considering, the *opportunities* that may be available to you as you pursue your goals, and your personal *strengths* that will help ensure your success. You may have come across this type of tool in your studies at school. Now it is time to apply it to your personal goals. What could be more important than your life and your success?

For each of your goals, consider the possible dangers, opportunities, and strengths carefully. While considering your goals, if you cannot think of possible dangers or opportunities on your own, you may want to ask a family member, a friend, or an outside expert. Asking someone you trust and whose opinion you respect will provide you with additional insight. Completing the DOS analysis, you may find the dangers of your plan are too great, or the opportunities too limited to make pursuing a particular goal worthwhile.

What are the Dangers, Opportunities, and Strengths (DOS) unique to you and your ability to achieve your goals? Taking a few minutes to complete Exercise 3 can pay off in the long run.

1.4 Step 4: Treasure it, recycle it, trash it

Step 4, "treasure it, recycle it, and trash it" is an examination of your current behaviors, and which ones prevent you from achieving your larger goals. Exercise 4 will help you learn new behaviors to "treasure," and help you "recycle" or "trash" behaviors that limit your success. By completing this exercise you will learn to modify your behavior.

As you reflect on your current situation and your goals, ask yourself the following questions:

- What needs to change?
- What am I currently doing which prevents me from moving forward?
- What will I treasure?
- Is there a better way to meet important goals?
- What needs to be recycled? (In other words, can you modify your behavior or goal to achieve a better result?)

EXERCISE 3
Dangers, Opportunities, and Strengths (DOS) Analysis

1. Dangers *(list the things that keep you awake at night worrying)*:
   _____
   _____
   _____
   _____
   _____

2. Opportunities *(list the things that excite you and inspire you to proceed)*:
   _____
   _____
   _____
   _____
   _____

3. Strengths *(list the things that help you sleep)*:
   _____
   _____
   _____
   _____
   _____

- What needs to be trashed? (What are you prepared to give up to meet an important goal?)
- Am I currently doing something that prevents me from reaching an important goal?

When completing the time frame and savings column, consider how much time is required to achieve your goals and how much money will be saved or required by pursuing a course of action. Clearly defining a time frame and allocation of dollars will increase your likelihood of completing the desired actions.

2. Examples of Goal Setting

Meet Matt. He enjoys team sports and is always ready to join in any fun. Besides sports, Matt loves to travel. His favorite saying is, "Just go with the flow."

Matt works as a server in a trendy bistro. It is a fun job and he is friends with the other servers. After work they like to check out some of the other hot spots in town. As a server, a large portion of his income comes in the form of tips. Often these are in cash and it is easy to lose track of how much he has in his pocket. Matt's income can be very sporadic. Some weeks Matt makes a lot of money, while other weeks, he has trouble making his rent. Because Matt lives in the moment, most of the time he has little savings, spending his income as it comes in on whatever catches his attention.

EXERCISE 4
Treasure It, Recycle It, Trash It

Treasure It	Recycle It	Trash It	Time Frame and Savings

Recently Matt has fallen in love with Cassie. She works for the local newspaper as the editor's assistant.

Cassie is curious about life and people in general. She is very curious about Matt. Recently Cassie asked Matt how much money he thought just slipped through his fingers each month. After a quick reflection on his past month of spending, Matt determined he was spending approximately $1,200 a month on fun.

Matt wants to purchase a brand new car, which is priced at $35,000. The problem is, Matt does not have any savings and would have to borrow the full $35,000. Taking out a five-year loan at 8 percent interest means payments would be approximately $700 a month. Having this much debt would cause even more problems with his cash flow. It might even prevent Matt from reaching his travel goals. Normally, Matt takes a last-minute travel special once a year, spending less than $1,000.

Matt loves to travel and his old friend Greg from high school is getting married next spring in Cancún. Matt has not seen Greg for several years and he has yet to meet Greg's fiancée. Matt thinks it would be fun to get reacquainted. The price (including travel, accommodation, and gift) for Matt to attend is $3,500. Matt asks Cassie if she would like to join him, but he knows Cassie is cautious with money. She cannot see herself paying so much to attend a wedding, and she doesn't want to dip into her savings or her emergency fund. If Matt goes, he will have to put the wedding on his charge card because he doesn't have any savings.

Clearly Matt does not have a strategy for achieving his goals, as seen on his first attempt at completing his Goals, Position, and Strategy (GPS) exercise.

SAMPLE 6
Matt's GPS Exercise

Areas to Consider	Goals What do you want most?	Position Today What is your current position?	Success Strategy What steps do you need to take for success?
Buy a car	Buy a brand new car. Cost: $35,000	No savings	?
Vacation	Go to Greg's wedding in Cancún. Cost: $3,500	No savings	?

Matt will need to complete the Dangers, Opportunities, and Strengths (DOS) analysis, and the treasure it, recycle it, trash it worksheets to help him consider his options. How might Matt modify his goals, and change the behaviors which prevent him from reaching his goals? Can Matt set himself up for financial security in the next six months?

SAMPLE 7
Matt's DOS Analysis

---

1. Dangers *(list the things that keep you awake at night worrying)*:
   - No savings.
   - Difficulty with cash flow. If I proceed with the car purchase and miss a payment, I could lose the car and hurt my credit rating.
   - A large car loan payment means little left over to achieve my other goals.
   - The car I want will be expensive to insure.
   - Spending money on unimportant things prevents me from reaching my car and travel goals.
   - Cassie is not impressed with my wild spending. I may lose her respect and love.

2. Opportunities *(list the things that excite you and inspire you to proceed)*:
   - I realize I could save a large portion of my income. I estimate that I spend between $1,200 and $1,500 a month that I cannot account for.
   - Rather than keep tips in my pocket I could deposit them in a bank account on my way home from work.

3. Strengths *(list the things that help you sleep)*:
   - I am easy going and well-liked by all. Because of my winning personality I usually get more tips than the other servers.
   - I am optimistic and hard working.

After completing the DOS Analysis, Matt is surprised to see how many dangers there are in his plan. To reach his goals he will need to change his current behaviors *and* modify his goals.

When Matt learned that his monthly car loan payments would be more than $700 a month he realized the best way to test his ability to make those payments was by saving that amount each and every month for six months. Clearly, if he failed at this savings plan, then he should not be buying the car! By implementing this saving plan, Matt will be able to put a deposit on his car, reducing his loan. By putting a savings plan in place Matt has learned he is capable of doing more with his income than he anticipated. He surprised himself with what he can accomplish.

Let's take a look at Sample 8.

Matt decides to forgo Greg's destination wedding. Instead he will take Greg and his fiancée for a dinner and give them a nice wedding gift of cash.

When Matt's car dealer told him that a one- to two-year old car of the same make and model could save him $7,000, he quickly realized that was equivalent to ten months of savings. Matt decided to purchase the used model with low mileage, and he still received all of the remaining new car warranties.

Matt upped the ante by choosing to be more careful with his tips, which were often in cash. By choosing to pass up on his late night excursions with the other servers he was able to save $470 a month. Matt was surprised to learn he did not

SAMPLE 8
Matt's Treasure It, Recycle It, Trash It Exercise

Goal: Greg's wedding

Treasure It	Recycle It	Trash It	Time Frame and Savings
	Modify goal: Take Greg and his fiancée for dinner and give them a nice gift of $175	Skip the wedding	**Savings:** $3,225 ($3,500 minus the cash gift and cost of the dinner)

Goal: Purchase a car

Treasure It	Recycle It	Trash It	Time Frame and Savings
Start savings plan **Savings:** $700 a month for six months			**Time Frame:** Six months later **Savings:** $4,200 for down payment on car
		Limit bar hopping after work, saving an additional $470 a month	**Time Frame:** Six months later **Savings:** $2,820
	Modify goal: Purchase a secondhand version of the same car **Savings:** $7,000		**Savings:** Price of secondhand car: $28,000 (Deposit $7,000 and borrow $21,000) Loan payment: $425 per month

miss these little treats and he was still able to keep his regular appointments with friends for a game of soccer, hockey, and his regular fitness routine.

Matt was rightfully proud to become the owner of his dream car. The monthly payments have dropped from the expected $700 a month to a more manageable $425. Matt continues to save $300 a month to his savings account. He deposits his tips on his way home from work keeping only what he needs for the next day.

Having savings in the bank means he no longer runs out of cash in a week when tips are low. By forgoing an expensive wedding holiday, which was outside of his ability to pay cash for, he has earned the respect of Cassie. They are now planning a getaway together for next year. Matt is thinking his next goal just might be an engagement ring!

By doing the exercises, Matt has discovered he is prepared to make changes to his current lifestyle in order to achieve his larger goals. By making a series of small sacrifices, he is able to gain control of his finances and has the ability to make wise choices.

There are many ways Matt could have achieved his goals — the samples include only a few. There is no single right answer.

Now, let's leave Matt for the moment. Next up is Sam's story.

Sam has just completed the visualization exercise and, in doing so, Sam has learned something important about himself. Although his parents have always hoped he would become a doctor, Sam realizes that his true passion is for animals. Sam grew up on a farm and he enjoys the wide open spaces and animals. He never wants to live in a big city. Every chance he has gotten over the past three years, he has been working at the animal shelter in town.

Sam is now ready to make several important decisions. He now begins work on the Goals, Position, and Strategy (GPS) exercise (see Sample 9) as well as completing the Dangers, Opportunities, and Strengths (DOS) analysis (see Sample 10).

Sam had hoped to move out of his family home this year and move into residence at the university. This would have allowed him to socialize with friends while completing his education. Now that Sam has completed the exercises, he realizes that the extra cost for residence would increase his student debt. Instead of staying in residence, he decides to stay at home with his folks. Sam's parents have offered him the use of the old pick-up truck so he can drive to school. On the days Sam studies late, he can stay with his older sister closer to the university.

In making the decision to switch from medicine to veterinary studies, Sam is now, more than ever, motivated to succeed. He realizes that if he can increase his grades, he may qualify for a scholarship. Sam decides to go for it. He now sees living at home as an advantage, since he will have more time for study and this may just provide the edge he needs to increase his marks. This will help Sam to graduate with less debt. This is important to Sam because his biggest goal of all is to have a veterinary practice of his own.

Sam realizes that if he can keep his debt down to $35,000, he will be able to pay back his debt within five years of graduating. Sam can do this by saving the money he makes working part time at the animal shelter to pay for a portion of his tuition.

As much as Sam would like to move to his own apartment as soon as he graduates, he realizes he may be better off staying with his parents for one more year. That way he can pay down a bigger portion of his student debt and still have enough left over to save up six months of salary to use for emergencies, as well as a deposit for his first and last month's rent.

Assuming Sam earns $60,000 in his first year as a veterinarian, he should be debt-free five years after graduating. Sam befriends his local banker, who tells him if he is unable to earn $60,000 in his first year and is forced to accept a position for much less money, his student loan could be amortized (paid off) over 15 years. This would drop the monthly payment to $267. However, the interest due over the course of the entire 15 years would jump to $24,734! Sam is very motivated to pay off his loan as quickly as possible!

If Sam can pay his loan off in five years as he plans, he will be in a better position to achieve his ten-year goal, which is opening his own clinic. Sam imagines the sign hanging in front of the office with his name on it!

Sam researches income for graduating veterinarians and discovers he can expect to make approximately $60,000 in his first year and his income could rise to $100,000 or more within ten years.

After completing the exercises, Sam is confident that he will be able to achieve his goals. Sam talks to his parents about his plans and is pleasantly surprised to find how supportive they are.

Sam shares his DOS analysis with his parents and guidance counselor. He is able to gain more insight from these conversations. One of the dangers he had not considered was what happens if there are already too many graduating veterinarians and too few jobs available when he graduates? This would limit his opportunities to obtain a full-time job. If this happens, it may be many years before he obtains a position and/or the pay scale may be reduced. Sam decides to discuss this with the veterinarians he has met through his part-time work. He could also discuss this with his guidance professional at the university. Having this conversation now, before he switches programs, could save Sam a lot of problems in the future.

Matt and Sam are well on their way. Now it is your turn. By completing the exercises included in this chapter, you will be able to gain a clear understanding of your personal short-, mid- and long-term goals for the next decade and the steps required to achieve your goals.

SAMPLE 9
Sam's GPS Exercise

Time Frame	Goals What do you want most?	Position Today What is your current position?	Success Strategy What steps do you need to take for success?
Years 2 to 4	**Education:** Graduate from university	University student completing an undergraduate school (majors: science and math)	Change direction of studies and move to a four-year veterinarian program
	Work with animals	Part-time work at an animal shelter	Continue to work at the shelter Ask boss to coach me and help me achieve my goals
Year 5	Career: Hired as a veterinarian	Student	Employer: To work for a veterinarian that is supportive of my goals Also to work for someone who is planning to retire within ten years of me being hired Salary (first year): $60,000
Years 5 to 10	Pay off student loans Pay off credit card debt	Current debt: $25,000 Estimated debt (upon graduation): $35,000	Control debt by living at home Apply for scholarships Pay debt over five years at 8 percent Annual payment: $8,490
Years 6 to 7	An apartment of my own overlooking an open field	Living at home with Mom and Dad	Graduate and secure a job. Live with parents for one year Save for deposit on apartment Save for emergencies
Year 10	Business of my own on Main Street Hang sign with my business name on it		Pay off student debt before opening my business Open savings account after graduation to save for my business

SAMPLE 10
Sam's DOS Analysis

1. Dangers *(list the things that keep you awake at night worrying)*:
   - I worry about not qualifying for a scholarship. *(If this happened, Sam would be forced to increase his debt load, causing him to postpone his goal of owning his own clinic.)*

2. Opportunities *(list the things that excite you and inspire you to proceed)*:
   - I am excited about the opportunities I have and that I will be exposed to by working at the animal shelter. I am in the perfect place to learn and gain the support of other veterinarians.
   - Working at the shelter now gives me the opportunity to meet potential employers and future clients.
   - The local veterinarian is aging and has told me she plans to retire in the next ten years. I could ask to be her assistant to gain experience in the clinic environment.

3. Strengths *(list the things that help you sleep)*:
   - I am focused, young, and energetic.
   - I am a good student.
   - My parents support my goals and they are willing to help with the use of their pick-up truck and a place to live while I achieve my dreams.
   - I am already employed in the industry I love. This provides me with many opportunities to learn from the pros.

CHAPTER SEVEN

Create a Budget

* Read this if you want to make informed choices about how you spend your money in the coming months and years.

* Read this if you are looking for ways to grow your money to meet future goals.

Your twenties are a time when you begin to discover what you want from life. For many in their twenties this means an active social life and fulfilling hobbies while pursuing educational and career goals.

If you find there are more things competing for your dollars than money coming into your bank account, you are not alone. A budget will help you to understand where your money is going so you can better allocate your dollars to meet your goals.

1. Needs and Wants

A three-year-old can be forgiven for claiming he *needs* Lego. Using his cutest smile, and a big hug, he may convince his mother of his need for Lego. At the age of 16 if he claims he *needs* a shiny new red

Corvette, his mother may tell him he *wants* a Corvette and if so, what does *he* plan to do about it?

What is the difference between a *want* and a *need*? Needs relate to your basic living requirements while wants are the things you would like to have or do, but which are not fundamental to your survival.

Ask yourself: "Can I survive without food, shelter, clothing, health care, and dental care?" The answer is no. These are your basic needs.

Now ask yourself: "Can I survive without my cell phone, Internet, a good education, and a means of transportation?" The answer this time may be "it depends." If you need your cell phone, access to the Internet, and a car for your job or even a job search, the answer is that these are indeed needs. At one time when preparing budgets for clients, a landline phone was considered a need. In today's world, you might say the cell phone is a need and the landline is simply a want. Also, since the cost of a good education with a well-thought-out career path will lead to financial security, it can be rightfully considered an investment in yourself.

Now ask yourself: "Do I need to go to the movies, dine out, have a gym membership, and go on expensive vacations? Do I need the newest video game, cell phone, and computer?" Clearly these are wants.

There is also a category called "frills," or what I like to call your "latte score." Do you need a daily double whipped cream mocha cappuccino? Are you a smoker? What about that tattoo you have been thinking about? Are you supporting your lifestyle with credit card debt? The higher your latte score, the less money you will be able to put toward your mid- and long-term savings goals. The attraction of the latte is instant gratification. Ask yourself, "Do I want this latte *more* than I want a shiny new car, my dream holiday, or a home of my own?" If you do this each time, instead of having that latte, cigarette, or tattoo, you may choose to walk right by and put the money into your car, holiday, or home savings account instead!

1.1 Control your spending

Can't control your spending? Let technology do it for you. There is a tool to help you cope with temptation. If you find yourself overspending on your wants, you may want to try MasterCard's inControl program and its company partner Citigroup. In a MasterCard news release it says, "inControl empowers customers to establish

QUIZ 1
What Is Your Latte Score?

Before you begin the quiz, add up the amount of money spent in the last week on wants and frills. What percentage does this represent of your take-home pay?

1. You are the first person in line to buy the newest technology (e.g., cell phone, computer, video games, TV). You know the price will drop within six months to a year, but you still want to be the first to own the latest toy. *(if you answer yes, add 10 points)*

2. You carry a balance on your credit cards and/or department store cards. *(if you answer yes, add 10 points)*

3. You make the minimum payment on your charge cards each month. *(if you answer yes, add 20 points)*

4. You find it difficult to save money each month. *(if you answer yes, add 10 points)*

5. You are a smoker. With the cost of a package of cigarettes around $10, smoking a pack a day is equal to $3,650 a year – literally your money has gone up in smoke! *(if you answer yes, add 50 points)*

6. You have $200 in your pocket, do you decide to go —

    • to your dentist for your semiannual checkup *(if you answer yes, 0 points)*, or
    • to a studio to get a tattoo *(if you answer yes, add 20 points)*?

7. Wants and frills as a percentage of your take-home pay includes money spent on hobbies, sports, video games, movies, coffee, muffins, take out and restaurant meals, magazines, etc. Now calculate what percentage this amount was of your last week's take-home pay:

    • Less than 7 percent: You are in control and know where your money is spent. *(if it is less than 7 percent, 0 points)*
    • 8 percent to 15 percent: You enjoy life's small pleasures and have a balanced budget. *(if it is in this range, add 10 points)*
    • 20 percent or higher: Where is your money going? This is a cause for concern. *(if you scored in the 20 percent or higher range, add 20 points)*

Take a few minutes to calculate your latte score. The higher your latte score, the harder it will be to build your wealth foundation!

    • 20 points or less: Your money knows who is boss!
    • 50 points or less: You are still in control.
    • 50 points or more: There is still time; review your budget for opportunities to change your spending habits.
    • 70 points or more: You could make better choices; review your spending and your habits.
    • 100 points or more: Drastic action is required; you are making poor decisions which will eventually catch up with you.

customized spend-management controls as well as maintain secure and intended usage through real-time alerts.[1]" The application allows you to set a ceiling on the amount of money that comes out of your account each month. Or maybe you just need a reminder when you are overspending. The inControl features include being able to:

---

[1] MasterCard, "Citi to Implement MasterCard inControl," www.mastercard.com, (2010), accessed June 2011.

- Set up and manage spending limits.

- Set up budgets for particular types of spending and manage exactly where, when, how, and for what types of purchases your credit cards may be used. For example, you can preset the amount of money you will allow yourself to spend in restaurants.

- Establish how and when you receive alerts (e.g., via SMS [text], or email) to safeguard against overspending and to keep you informed in real time about attempted card activity.

2. Budgeting to Live within Your Means

Budgeting does not mean giving up all your wants. With a well-planned budget you are aware of the difference between needs, wants, and frills so you may better choose how to allocate your money leading you to your most important goals. When you create your own personalized budget you will learn how to prioritize your money in the following order:

1. Financial obligations and savings

2. Needs

3. Allocate surplus to your wants

2.1 The lifestyle your income will support

Have you ever wondered about the lifestyle of someone you admire? What does the person earn and how does he or she afford his or her current lifestyle? The following sections include five examples that may help you to put a cost to the lifestyles you admire. Or, better yet, help you to understand what your income will support. The first two lifestyles may represent your early career days. If you are fortunate, the last three lifestyles may be representative of your later career years. (Note that each lifestyle is based on an *after*-tax income.)

2.1a A simple life

Annual income: $25,000 for a single person and $40,000 for a couple (see Exercise 7)

The simple life provides a modest rental apartment in a small town or a shared apartment in a large city. Your rent is your single largest monthly expense. Depending on where you live, you may have difficulty finding rental accommodation that is within the recommended 30 percent of your income.[2]

You take public transportation, or use a bicycle to get around. Much of your time is spent with family and friends who live nearby. Your hobbies will be modest such as walking or biking. You are a member at the YMCA, and may qualify for a reduced membership fee. Most of your budget is spent on your needs, and your wants are modest; dining out and going to the movies are a treat. You are proud of your ability to buy what you need on sale.

2.1b A simple comfortable life

Annual income: $45,000 for a single person and $60,000 for a couple (see Exercise 8)

The simple comfortable life provides a reasonable rental apartment in a medium-sized city. Your rent is likely in the range of $1,100 to $1,800 a month. If you have a vehicle, it is an older model, or you take public transportation.

Free time and little money are spent with family and friends. Your hobbies may include skiing, biking, or perhaps a gym membership. Your income allows for an annual vacation, perhaps a last-minute cruise or a sun destination costing $1,000 to $1,300. Most of your budget is spent on your needs, but you are still able to dine out or go to the movies on occasion. You like to search for specials and other discounts to extend your entertainment and travel budget.

2.1c Above average

Annual income: $60,000 for a single person and $95,000 for a couple (see Exercise 9)

The above average lifestyle provides a comfortable apartment, a small condo in the city, or a perhaps a home of your own in the suburbs. Your housing costs are likely $1,800 to $2,500 a month. You may have a recent model vehicle, which was leased or purchased with a loan.

In your free time you enjoy entertaining. Your hobbies are varied and you enjoy a gym membership. Your income allows for an annual vacation or perhaps a few weekends in the country at a nice hotel

---

[2] Tony Pugh, "Recession takes severe toll on low-income renters," www.mcclatchydc.com, (February 1, 2011), accessed June 2011.

and spa. You take advantage of last-minute travel specials to stretch your travel budget.

Your budget allows you to spend on your needs and your wants, and you are able to set money aside to save for future needs as well. You do not like to "tip the tax man" so you make the maximum contribution to your retirement plans which reduces your taxes. By all means, tip your server, hairdresser, and cab driver, but try not to tip the tax man! We all have an obligation to pay our fair share of taxes, but pay more taxes than you need to and you are effectively giving the tax man a tip. Take advantage of the tax breaks available to you!

2.1d Luxury

Annual income: $80,000 for a single person and $135,000 for a couple

The luxury lifestyle provides a luxury condo in the city or perhaps a home of your own. Your housing costs are likely $2,500 to $3,800 a month. You have a recent model vehicle, and may have a second vehicle.

In your free time you enjoy entertaining either at home or in restaurants. Your hobbies may include skiing, golf, and a gym membership. Your yearly vacations may include a two-week holiday to the isles of Greece or perhaps bushwhacking in Tunisia.

Your budget allows you to comfortably spend on your needs and your wants, and you are able to set money aside to save for future needs as well. You make the maximum contribution to your retirement plans each and every year.

2.1e Prestige

Annual income: $115,000 for a single person and $185,000 for a couple

The prestige lifestyle provides you with your dream home, and maybe a condo in cottage country. Your housing costs are likely $4,000 to $5,800 a month. You have a new car, and a second recent-model vehicle.

On summer weekends you can be found at your condo on the lake, and in winter you plan your three-week vacations in the sunny south. You and your friends enjoy tennis, golf, and swimming at a fantastic country club.

You set aside money each and every month, saving for your future needs, such as a second home or retirement. You make the maximum contribution to your retirement plans each and every year.

2.2 Create and follow a budget

Rate your effectiveness as the boss of your money:

- **Did the money you earned last month exceed your expenses?** If your expenses are more than your income, you are living beyond your means and it will not be long before you are miserable. You need to cut back. By creating and sticking to a budget you will show your money who is boss, which will make you happy.

- **How much was left over at the end of the month?** If you have extra cash each month, you can use it to build a nest egg to fund a future purchase or save a portion for your long-term goals.

A simple cash flow statement does not take much time to set up and it can help you see where there may be opportunities to reduce costs. You will need a calculator, a pad of paper, and a pencil to complete the cash flow exercises.

- **Calculate your income:** Add up your income for the year and calculate a monthly average (see Exercise 5).

- **Track your expenses:** Collect your household's bank statements and bills and then record your expenses in categories such as those listed in Exercise 6. This will help you to identify where your money is going and how much you are spending monthly.

- **It is a good idea to record all of your out-of-pocket expenses for the following month.** The easiest way to do this is to take $20 to $40 at the beginning of each week and then use your debit card for all other expenses. That way when you review your bank statement all of your expenditures will be showing.

Before you begin, gather the following information and documents:

- Payroll/income slips from all sources showing income and deductions.

- Bank statements — an important source of information for debit card expenses, income sources, and regular bill payments.

- Credit card statements.

- Loan payments (e.g., loan statements, credit card, student loan, department store).

- Rent or mortgage payments, property tax, utility bills, and parking and condo or strata fees.

- Car expenses including loan payment, insurance, gas, and maintenance bills.

- Insurance costs including home insurance, health insurance, and life and disability premiums.

- Cash expenditures — if you pay cash for out-of-pocket expenses you will need to track what you spend your cash on for at least one month.

- Clothing expenses.

- Don't forget those once-a-year charges such as income taxes owed for the previous year and property tax, birthday and Christmas gifts, and vacation expenses. Divide these by 12 to create a monthly cost.

Once you have collected all of your documents, it is time to complete the following exercises. This will show you how much cash flows into and out of your accounts each month and where you are spending your money.

EXERCISE 5
Cash Flow Statement: Income

Income Per Month	Total
Net employment income	
Government benefits	
Tips	
Bonuses	
Gifts	
Other	
Total Income from All Sources	

Multiply your monthly income from Exercise 5 by 12 to calculate your annual income. Use this information to select the typical budget exercise for you discussed in section **2.3**.

Using Exercise 6, fill in your monthly expenses.

EXERCISE 6
Cash Flow Statement: Expenses

Expenses Per Month	Monthly Cost		Expenses Per Month	Monthly Cost
Needs				
Housing			*Financial Obligations*	
Rent or mortgage			Saving for retirement plans	
Condo fees			Saving for goals	
Utilities (e.g., heat, hydro)			Pension contributions	
Phone, Internet, cable			Loan payments	
Property insurance			Credit card payments	
Property tax			Health insurance	
Repairs and maintenance			Life insurance	
Other			Disability insurance	
Total Housing Expenses			**Total Financial Obligations**	
Transportation			*Daily Living*	
Bus, train, and cabs			Groceries	
Car loan payment			Clothing	
Vehicle insurance			Grooming	
Gas			Other	
Maintenance and parking			Other	
Total Transportation Expenses			**Total Daily Living Expenses**	
Health Care				
Eyes				
Dental				
Prescriptions				
Other				
Total Health Care Expenses				
Wants				
Frills			*Miscellaneous*	
Fitness			Gifts	
Dining out (also include daily lattes, etc.)			Charities	
Hobbies			Other	
Pets				
Travel				
Subscriptions				
Other				
Total Frills			**Total Miscellaneous**	
			Total Expenses for All Sources	
			Monthly Balance/Shortfall	

To calculate your monthly cash flow balance, simply subtract *total expenses from all sources* from *total income from all sources*.

Multiply your monthly expenses by 12 to calculate your annual expenses. Use this information to compare how you are doing on the typical budget exercise designed for you in section **2.3**.

2.3 Typical budget

Now that you have completed your income and expense exercises, you have a clear idea of where your money is going each month. Are you happy with your results? Or would you like to improve your money management skills?

In these next few pages you will learn how to adjust your budget to meet *all* of your needs and wants in a prudent fashion. After all, the purpose of a budget is to ensure you have allocated funds to all of the important areas of your life.

The exercises that follow provide examples of budgets for various income categories. To use these exercises you will need to multiply your monthly costs for each category by 12 to arrive at the annual expense. Now find the exercise which best represents your current annual income. Enter your costs and compare how you are doing to how a typical prudent person might allocate his or her funds.

Exercise 7 reflects a simple and modest lifestyle of someone earning $25,000 to $40,000. This person has little room for savings and must budget carefully to meet his or her needs. Exercise 8 provides a more comfortable lifestyle for those earning $45,000 to $60,000, and for those who are saving for future goals. Exercise 9 is typical of the above average lifestyle in the earning range of $60,000 to $95,000. This person can meet his or her savings and financial goals while enjoying a comfortable lifestyle.

The following sections explain how to complete the exercises.

2.3a Financial obligations

The financial obligations section of Exercises 7, 8, and 9 is where you will record the money you are saving to reach goals, payments made toward reducing your debts, and any insurance premiums.

- **Savings toward goals:** Record the amount of money you are contributing monthly toward your various savings goals. Pay yourself first[3]; reach your goals by making saving your first priority. You will be more likely to save if the first thing you do when you get paid is transfer the money you want to save from your bank account directly into accounts you have set up for your goals. If you don't see your savings dollars sitting in your bank account, you won't think about them or miss them, and your spending habits will adjust accordingly. The risk of leaving your savings money in your checking account is that the money needed for savings can be too easily spent on your current wants.

- **Insurance:** Record the premiums you pay for your health, disability, and life insurance.

- **Loan payments:** If you have debt from student loans and/or credit cards, here is where you record your monthly payments. Exercises 7, 8, and 9 assume you are able to satisfy your lenders by applying 8 percent of your income toward debt reduction. You may be able to increase or reduce your allocation to debt repayment as your situation warrants.

2.3b Needs

The big items in this section of the exercise are your costs related to food, shelter, and transportation.

- **Food:** Depending on your lifestyle, the exercises allow for $55 to $90 per week toward groceries for an adult. If there is more than one person in your household, you will need to increase the food budget for each additional person by $60 per week. Add $3,120 a year for each additional adult in your household and roughly half that amount for each child.

- **Shelter:** This category includes costs associated with your rent and parking (if applicable). If you own a home, include the cost of your mortgage as well as the principal and interest plus the property taxes and condo/strata fees (if any).

- **Utilities:** Record your costs for hydro, heat, and water.

- **Technology:** This category includes costs for your phone (i.e., cell phone and/or land line), Internet, and cable fees. These fees can vary. The costs for these services are to a large degree within your control, but can easily get out of control. For many

---

[3] David Chilton, *The Wealthy Barber*, Stoddart Publishing Co. Limited, 1989.

people this is a category in which money simply slips away in user fees. Look closely at your technology fees and ask yourself: "Am I getting good value for the dollars spent?"

- **Transportation:** Record your costs for transportation. If you bike or use public transit, estimate the monthly cost. If you own or lease a vehicle, add up your monthly payments. Remember to include the cost of gas, insurance, and regular maintenance.

- **Clothing, health care, and grooming:** In these three categories record the costs for your personal care. This is another area where savvy shoppers find opportunities for savings.

2.3c Wants

Now that you have recorded all of your financial obligations and needs, how much is left over? The cash that is left over each month can now be allocated to your *wants*. The following budget exercises will give you some ideas for the distribution of your cash towards your wants, but it is up to you. You may prefer to allocate more to movies and entertainment and less to fitness. Or you may have an expensive pet, and are willing to forgo vacations. Once you have completed your personalized budget, compare how you are doing:

- Do you have a well-balanced approach to budgeting?

- Are you saving money each month for your mid- and long-term goals?

- Are you meeting all of your needs with enough left over to meet your wants, or is your rent too expensive? Does your vehicle cost a lot to maintain? Are these costs preventing you from enjoying life?

Now is the time to examine your income and expenses to see where you can make changes to better meet your goals. After all, you are the driver of your financial life plan, so take control and enjoy a balanced budget.

Choose the exercise that best matches your net employment income. Net employment income (can also be described as "take-home pay") is the amount you receive after your employer deducts taxes, benefits, and other costs. For example, if your net employment income is $45,000 per year use Exercise 8.

EXERCISE 7
Simple Lifestyle Budget

Typical Budget Allocations $25,000 to $40,000	Simple Lifestyle Budget	%	Compare How are you doing?
Financial Obligations			
Savings toward goals	$600	2.0%	
Insurance (e.g., life, health, and disability premiums)	1,500	5.0	
Loan payments (e.g., student loan, credit cards)	2,400	8.0	
Needs			
Food	3,450	11.5	
Shelter (e.g., rent, mortgage, condo fees, interest, taxes, insurance)	9,000	30.0	
Utilities (e.g., heat, hydro)	2,700	9.0	
Technology (e.g., cell phone, landline, cable, Internet)	1,200	4.0	
Transportation (e.g., bus, train, and car — loan payment, insurance, gas, maintenance)	3,000	10.0	
Clothing	1,050	3.5	
Health care	900	3.0	
Grooming	300	1.0	
Wants			
Hobbies, sports, gym membership	450	1.5	
Miscellaneous (e.g., furniture, appliances, TV, computer)	900	3.0	
Entertainment (e.g., movies, dining out)	900	3.0	
Travel/Holidays	600	2.0	
Daily cash (e.g., coffee)	750	2.5	
Gifts and contributions	300	1.0	
Total Expenditures	**$30,000**	**100%**	

EXERCISE 8
Simple Comfortable Lifestyle Budget

Typical Budget Allocations $45,000 to $60,000	Comfortable Lifestyle Budget	%	Compare How are you doing?
Financial Obligations			
Savings toward goals	$3,675	7.0%	
Insurance (e.g., life, health, and disability premiums)	2,100	4.0	
Loan payments (e.g., student loan, credit cards)	4,200	8.0	
Needs			
Food	3,412	6.5	
Shelter (e.g., rent, mortgage, condo fees, interest, taxes, insurance)	15,750	30.0	
Utilities (e.g., heat, hydro)	3,675	7.0	
Technology (e.g., cell phone, landline, cable, Internet)	1,575	3.0	
Transportation (e.g., bus, train, and car — loan payment, insurance, gas, maintenance)	6,825	13.0	
Clothing	1,575	3.0	
Health care	788	1.5	
Grooming	525	1.0	
Wants			
Hobbies, sports, gym membership	1,575	3.0	
Miscellaneous (e.g., furniture, appliances, TV, computer)	1,575	3.0	
Entertainment (e.g., movies, dining out)	1,575	3.0	
Travel/Holidays	1,575	3.0	
Daily cash (e.g., coffee)	1,050	2.0	
Gifts and contributions	1,050	2.0	
Total Expenditures	**$52,500**	**100%**	

EXERCISE 9
Above Average Lifestyle Budget

Typical Budget Allocations $65,000 to $95,000	Above Average Lifestyle Budget	%	Compare How are you doing?
Financial Obligations			
Savings toward goals	$7,750	10.0%	
Insurance (e.g., life, health, and disability premiums)	3,100	4.0	
Loan payments (e.g., student loan, credit cards)	6,200	8.0	
Needs			
Food	3,488	4.5	
Shelter (e.g., rent, mortgage, condo fees, interest, taxes, insurance)	23,638	30.5	
Utilities (e.g., heat, hydro)	3,875	5.0	
Technology (e.g., cell phone, landline, cable, Internet)	1,938	2.5	
Transportation (e.g., bus, train, and car — loan payment, insurance, gas, maintenance)	10,463	13.5	
Clothing	2,325	3.0	
Health care	775	1.0	
Grooming	1,163	1.5	
Wants			
Hobbies, sports, gym membership	1,938	2.5	
Miscellaneous (e.g., furniture, appliances, TV, computer)	2,325	3.0	
Entertainment (e.g., movies, dining out)	2,713	3.5	
Travel/Holidays	2,325	3.0	
Daily cash (e.g., coffee)	1,934	2.5	
Gifts and contributions	1,550	2.0	
Total Expenditures	**$77,500**	**100%**	

3. Seize Savings Opportunities

There are many ways to reduce expenses in a monthly budget. The most obvious is to eliminate frills; for example, consider whether you need to buy a latte and muffin on the way to work, when you could just as easily have breakfast at home. The cost of one latte and a muffin are equivalent to a box of cereal which will last more than a week! If you still want to share the morning camaraderie with your peers, order a small coffee instead.

How about your technology fees? When was the last time you compared the rates you are paying to current rates? Is it possible to renegotiate with your current provider or a competitor? Many providers offer discounts when you use them for all of your technology fees; bundling your phone, cable, and Internet with a single provider can save you many dollars a month.

4. Examples of Financial Lifestyles

Before we check in on Cassie, Matt, and Sam, consider the difference between "affluent" and "wealthy."

Affluent describes the person who passes money from hand to hand, purchasing the symbols of wealth, and leaving little left over to actually build wealth. People who like to live an affluent lifestyle may allocate more of their budget to their needs and wants such as high rent, expensive vehicles, designer clothing, and tech toys. This can mean there is little left over for saving toward future goals. They attempt to spend on both needs and wants to excess and can easily end up with a high level of debt. Soon the cost of carrying this debt will reduce their lifestyle. Matt, in section **4.2**, could be described as someone who is interested in an affluent lifestyle. He will need to take care to live within his means.

Wealthy describes the person who accumulates money to purchase the assets that create income so that working for a living becomes optional. Those who pursue wealth may choose to reduce their allocations to both needs and wants in order to save for their future goals such as purchasing a home, starting and running a business, or saving for their retirement. Sam, in section **4.3**, is a good example of someone who is planning to become wealthy and is prepared to delay the purchase of expensive lifestyle items in favor of building a foundation of wealth.

4.1 Cassie's financial life plan

Annual income: $35,000

Annual expenditures: $34,765

Result: Happiness

Cassie is prepared to live a modest, simple lifestyle in exchange for more security. Security for Cassie comes in the form of a stable job with benefits, money in the bank, and living within her means.

Cassie's life passions outside of work include bicycling and photography. She is frequently seen racing around town on her bike with a camera slung over her shoulder. Her social life revolves around the friends she has made in the cycling club which meets each Saturday morning for a race to the top of the local mountain and back. Sundays are spent with family — Mom makes a big dinner and sends Cassie back to her apartment with leftovers.

Cassie loves her single-room loft apartment located directly above the bike repair shop. It bears her signature eclectic flair and is filled with her grandmother's furnishings from the 1970s, movie posters, and a collection of antique cameras gathered from local antique shops. Her job is located just down the street so there is no need for a vehicle. Cassie takes public transportation or rides her bike.

She likes to share in the morning camaraderie at the local coffee shop with her peers, and will order a large tea which costs the same as a small coffee. Cassie has to hold back a smile when she listens to her latte-sipping friends complain about their credit card bills and general money problems. With a healthy bank balance and a growing emergency fund, Cassie has confidence that wealth does not always look like affluence. She is in good financial shape on a modest income yet she is the one walking out of the coffee shop with an extra $4 in her pocket.

Cassie's budget looks a lot like the typical budget for a person earning $35,000 with one large exception: Cassie continues to top up her student loan payments devoting $7,500 a year toward debt reduction, or 21 percent of her take-home pay. Doing so requires a reduction in the amount of money allocated to other areas of her budget. Not owning a vehicle saves Cassie thousands of dollars a year.

Cassie's employer offers a benefits package providing health, dental, life, and short-term disability insurance. Cassie worries about an accident or illness which would prevent her from working, so she purchases a long-term disability plan of her own.

Cassie's success tips are simple:

- Cassie sets up two separate accounts at her local bank, and names each account:

- The first account is for her monthly savings, loan obligations, and needs. She deposits $1,800 which is enough to cover her basic cost for savings, loan payment, insurance, rent, and technology. All of these are on automatic withdrawal payment. Cassie does not have a debit card for this account.

- The second account Cassie uses to make purchases for her daily living such as food, transportation, grooming, clothing, and wants. She uses her debit card to make these purchases so she can track where the money went.

- She avoids using her credit cards. When she does use her credit card, she makes sure to pay the balance in full before the due date.

- Cassie protects her valuables, especially her income, with insurance.

- When Cassie dines out, she chooses the least expensive item on the menu and saves 20 to 30 percent on her restaurant bill.

- When at the coffee shop, Cassie orders a small coffee or a large tea. This saves her more than 50 percent compared to the cost of a latte. Cassie calculates that over the next five years she will have $5,000 in savings simply by depositing the $73 a month she saves on lattes into an investment account earning 6 percent a year![4]

- Cassie never, ever pays full price! She waits for sales or she will negotiate. Often she will surf the net to get the best deals. Cassie's starting point is whether she can save 50 to 75 percent. She does the following:

  - Controls technology costs by shopping around for the best deal.

  - Shops for clothes at the end of the season and saves 50 percent or more.

  - Shops for vintage clothing and household goods at consignment shops, which saves her 70 percent or more.

Cassie is happy with her income and lifestyle. Her one indulgence is "Prints," a black Labrador retriever she rescued from the city animal shelter. She is proud of her ability to live within her means and with her growing savings account, she will soon be able to start looking for a condo of her own.

Her employer is giving her more responsibilities. Recently she has been asked to screen potential stories for the local news. Dr. Sam Fairly submitted a press release to Cassie's office announcing the opening of his new practice. Not only is Dr. Fairly the brains behind the volunteer horse rescue group called "St. Francis's Horses," at age 28 he is purchasing the veterinary practice of the retiring Dr. Wright. Cassie is intrigued; Dr. Fairly is only a few years older than her so how is

---

[4] Eisi, "NaviPlan Select Financial Planning Software," www.eisi.com/products/cdn/select/index.htm, (2010), accessed June 2011.

he so successful? She smells a story. Cassie finds herself thinking about Dr. Sam Fairly, so she does a web search. Is it possible that Dr. Sam Fairly could be the scrawny and overserious Samuel Fairly with the bad haircut, from high school?

Cassie gets permission to borrow a company car and a camera so she can go onsite and conduct an interview. She can hardly wait to tell Matt about her first interview! Matt has invited Cassie over for a home cooked meal later this week; he hinted he had some news for her.

4.2 Matt's financial life plan

Annual income: $35,000

Annual expenditure: $36,000

Result: Misery

Last time we spoke to Matt he was feeling pretty good. Why not? He has a love interest, a new car, and a savings plan. Six months later, as he was preparing for the next shot during a late night hockey game with the boys, Matt was slammed against the boards resulting in a broken ankle. His doctor ordered him to take six weeks off work. This was going to cost $3,300 in lost income alone! Matt had previously given little thought to what might happen to his finances in the event of an illness or accident. Now he realizes how exposed he is. His fixed costs for the next six weeks are $2,800. The restaurant where Matt works does not offer a health and disability plan, and he doesn't have insurance of his own. Matt will be forced to use the $1,800 in his savings account and will still be short $1,000, forcing him to draw cash from his credit card. This is a costly solution since the interest rate charged is 28 percent. Matt is not happy about adding to his credit card debt which is already at $5,000. Once he is back at work, he will have to work extra shifts to catch up. It will likely take Matt one year of working overtime to recover his lost income and savings.

He realizes he needs to plan better for the future and the unexpected. Matt is now thinking about his life more seriously. In the past, Matt's life was one big party, an adventure just waiting to be discovered a day at a time. He has been living to the maximum his income would allow. His budget has been out of control, with a latte score of 70.

The solution is simple: Reduce his lifestyle to fit his budget or increase his income to meet his needs and wants. Matt could keep his current job as a server and buy insurance to protect himself in the event of an accident or illness. This is a good plan and would lead to a more secure future, but Matt has a better idea. He asks himself: "What do I need to do to increase my income so that it meets the lifestyle I want?"

After Matt heals from his injury, he returns to work. On his third day back at work Matt helps Brad, the liquor wholesaler, stock shelves. Matt decides to ask Brad about his job and discovers the winery that Brad represents is looking to expand.

Before Brad can become regional manager, his company needs to hire a territory sales representative to take his place. Matt is curious, and interested. The compensation package offered by the winery includes a salary of $40,000 plus bonuses. Brad tells Matt he could expect to earn more than $45,000 per year plus a health and income benefits plan.

As the regional sales manager Brad expects to earn more than $70,000. Brad is planning to take courses to become a sommelier. Successful completion could add another $30,000 to his regional manager's salary of $70,000 for a total income of $100,000. Now Matt is excited, he can see by Brad's example a clear path to increasing his own income in the coming years with a solid career path.

Matt applies and gets this new position. He expects to earn $45,000, which is $10,000 more than his last year's earnings as a server. This gives Matt a lot of peace of mind. As long as he controls his costs, it will now be easy to meet his monthly expenses and his savings goals. A big bonus is that Matt will now be covered for health and disability benefits.

Brad tells Matt that an important part of the job is the use of his car to meet clients. The cost of operating Matt's car now becomes a tax deduction providing a tax savings of approximately $1,800 each year. Matt's new employer would pay for Matt's costs to entertain clients and potential clients as long as Matt submits an expense report with details of who he was out with and the potential for new business. Matt has always been eager to make new friends and learn from others to makes lifestyle changes to meet his goals. He can hardly believe his good fortune; this is the ideal career for him. He can hardly wait to tell Cassie his news.

Matt's success tips include many opportunities for change:

- Matt is prepared to sacrifice certainty of income to take jobs where his personal efforts impact his pay. He is confident of his ability to provide superior service that will result in tips, commissions, and bonuses. Matt is also prepared to work added hours to meet his income goals.

- Matt considers going back to school. He's intrigued by the idea of becoming a sommelier and is encouraged about how this credential can add thousands of dollars to his future income.[5]

- Matt takes advantage of tax breaks by writing off his car and technology expenses, which saves him 15 to 30 percent on his transportation and technology budget.

- While Matt was recuperating from his broken ankle he decided to learn to cook. He invited the cook at the restaurant where he works to come over and show him how. Matt is amazed at how much less expensive cooking is compared to dining out. The steak dinner served in the restaurant for $25

---

[5] Corie Brown, "So You Want to Be a Sommelier?," www.latimes.com/features/la-fo-sommeliers12dec12,0,5618925.story, (2007), accessed June 2011.

to $50 can be prepared at home for $7 to $10! A big bonus for Matt is the opportunity to entertain friends and show off his new skills.

- Matt commits to saving his tax refund each year. Because he does not receive the tax refund until after his tax returns are completed and returned to him, Matt will receive his tax refund in one lump sum. He commits to putting this money into his savings account for his long-term goals.

- Matt knows that if money is in his bank account he will spend it, so he —

  - sets up an automatic banking withdrawal, which transfers the amount he wants to save each month to a savings account at a different bank. This makes it easier to withstand temptation;

  - pays his car insurance monthly, rather than semiannually. This way he does not have to worry about a big bill once a year; and

  - puts $80 a month towards his vacation account. Now he has the savings on hand to pay for a holiday when he is ready to travel.

- Matt puts his credit cards in the freezer in a large block of ice. He realizes if he has to wait for them to thaw, he might just change his mind, avoiding an impulse purchase!

After recovering from the setback with his broken ankle, Matt is beginning to feel more in control. He has learned the importance of protecting his lifestyle during an emergency. He has also discovered he has the potential to do much more with his life than he had previously thought. He will no longer allow the lack of a university degree to prevent him from achieving his ambitions. He can improve his credentials and employment opportunities by taking educational programs while working. Matt is discovering that school may have judged him by his marks, but life judges him by his accomplishments.

People who have ambition and drive often resist jobs with a fixed salary. They prefer and often choose jobs with compensation packages which reward them for their results. This includes sales positions that offer commissions and bonuses. This way, they can control their income because the harder they work, the more successful they become. However, people with a variable income need to plan their budget carefully. In the event of a downturn, they need to be able to reduce their expenses. It is a good idea to build and keep an emergency fund equivalent to six months' pay. This way if sales decline for a few months, they will be able to keep up with their expenses.

If Matt's earnings can stay ahead of his expenses, he will achieve happiness.

4.3 Sam's financial life plan

Cassie relaxes and feels the pressures of the city slip away, as she drives first the highways and then the rural roads to meet Dr. Fairly out in the country village of Caledon. She wonders what happened to the serious kid from high school.

Cassie recognizes the driveway she is looking for by the freshly painted sign on the gate: "Dr. Sam Fairly, Veterinarian." She is shocked to see the handsome young man who greets her. He reminds her she was in the tenth grade the year he finished his twelfth.

They do a quick tour of the office before getting into the interview. Cassie learns that Sam always has a five-year plan and he sticks to it. He is the driver of his life — organized and focused, with great follow-through skills. He is prepared to make short-term sacrifices for long-term gains. Sam's philosophy: "Life is long, be prepared to take calculated risks that will lead directly to your long-term goals." Sam is generous and supportive of his friends and neighbors. He expects the best of people and is seldom disappointed.

How did Sam transition so quickly from graduation to business owner? Sam tells Cassie how he has been working toward this day for the past five years. While studying for his doctorate he worked part time at the animal shelter. At the same time he founded the charitable organization "St. Francis's Horses" and encouraged local businesses and wealthy farmers to support the cause of finding good homes for horses that had been abandoned. During the summer months Sam helped Dr. Wright during her late-night emergency visits to local farmers assisting in births and other large animal care. Sam is now well-known in this small village as a young man with a strong commitment to his community. More important, he is well respected and well liked. A good reputation will help him grow his practice.

As Dr. Wright made her retirement plans, it did not take her long to recognize that Sam was a natural successor. Sam and Dr. Wright agreed on a transition plan whereby Sam will buy Dr. Wright's practice over the next five years. This means that Sam will have to assume $200,000 in debt on top of the $35,000 in student loans for a total of $235,000. His annual loan costs will be $24,000, or 30 percent of his income. This is a lot of money, but Sam has done his homework and is confident that if he is very careful, he will be able to repay his loans, giving himself a solid start to wealth accumulation. Since the banks won't lend Sam $200,000 at this stage of his career, Dr. Wright agrees to fund the sale, provided Sam can commit to paying the loan in full over the next five years. Sam will rent Dr. Wright's office until the end of the five-year term, after which he plans to buy the building from Dr. Wright. This suits Dr. Wright as it assures her of a source of retirement income for many years to come.

Cassie asks Sam; "What gives you the confidence you can carry such a high level of debt?" and "Isn't all debt bad?" Sam smiles, he agrees that debt can be bad, but when it is used to purchase something with an increasing value, debt can be a very good thing. He explains to Cassie that he was prepared to take on the loan for Dr. Wright's business because he believes the practice will grow in value and he is confident of his ability to pay his loan obligations on time. If Sam were to go into business on his own, without buying Dr Wright's practice, he would have to buy all of his own equipment, rent an office, hire an assistant, and build his business over time. It would take much longer than five years to reach the income Sam expects to make in his first year.

Sam explains to Cassie that in the past five years Dr. Wright's practice has grossed an average of $200,000 a year. After Sam pays $86,000 in operating costs for office expenses, $30,000 in wages for Dr Wright's long-time assistant, and $24,000 to cover the cost of the loan, Sam expects to make $60,000 a year. If he is careful, he will be able to save $80,000 over the next five years, which he can use towards a deposit on the office building owned by Dr. Wright. Sam says he's right on target with his five-year plan.

In the next five years Sam expects to increase the gross revenue of his business by 50 percent for a total of $300,000. By then, Sam calculates his own personal income will be well in excess of $100,000 per year. Cassie is impressed by how well thought out Sam's plan is.

Sam's success tips include being in control of his life plan:

- Sam has a plan and he's not afraid to tell the world. Sam updates his five-year plan regularly, and measures his progress annually.

- Sam sticks to a budget and he is prepared to make sacrifices in the short term to achieve outstanding results in the long term. Sam chooses to spend little on his needs and wants in order to focus on his savings and wealth-development goals.

- He assumes strategic debt, meaning the debt he takes on will lead to wealth.

- He avoids consumer debt such as credit cards. Sam is still driving his parents' old pick-up truck.

- Sam networks, which allows people to be as good to him as he has been to them. He lets people know what he is trying to accomplish.

- He looks for ways to give back to a community that has helped him get to where he is.

Cassie is happy with her interview and is excited to return to the office to write her story. She takes some final photos and is saying goodbye when Sam leans into the car and says: "Thank you Cassie, I sure am glad you came to see me today but I have a confession to make. You see, I remembered you from high school, so when I mailed in that press release, I was hoping you would be the one who came to interview me. If you hadn't, I would have had to call you. I really enjoyed getting to know you again after all these years. May I call you when I get into the city? Maybe we could go out for a nice lunch?"

Cassie has a lot to think about on the drive home. Did she understand Sam correctly? If she did, it looks like he has more than finances in his five-year plan. She is not sure how much of today's events she will share with Matt.

Cassie eventually goes on a few lunch dates with Sam and she finds that she really connects with him. After a few of these dates, and with mixed emotions, Cassie decides to go visit her grandmother, something she always does when life seems too confusing.

CHAPTER EIGHT

Calculate Your Net Worth

* Read this if you want to know how you are doing today and in the years to come.

* Read this if your banker wants to see your net worth statement before he or she will lend you money.

What is net worth and how do you measure it? The formula is simple:

Assets - Liabilities = Net Worth

Assets can best be described as the dollar value of the sum total of all your possessions and money due to you. Liabilities is the sum total of the money you owe to others.

Measuring your net worth tells you how wealthy you are. Updating your net worth statement each and every year will show you how quickly you are becoming wealthy. If you have a bad year, your updated net worth statement may inspire you to correct bad habits.

1. Examples of Net Worth

Let's begin by checking in on Matt and Cassie to see their calculations for their net worth. By seeing their examples, it will be easier to calculate your net worth in section **3**.

It has been six months since Matt bought his car. Recently he's had a string of bad days at his new job. He is frustrated and imagines how nice it would be to escape. He dreams about taking off on a five-year trip with *National Geographic* to the Pacific Ocean to swim with the whales and study marine life. He would be responsible for paying his own way, so it could get expensive; however, Matt considers it a trip of a lifetime.

First of all, Matt will need some money. He wonders how much he is worth. He sits down with a paper and pencil to plot his escape. His plans for the trip include raising as much money as possible. First he would have to empty his savings account and sell everything he owns.

He wouldn't be coming back for quite some time so he would have to quit his job. What will Matt's last paycheck look like? He has some vacation pay owed to him. There is no company pension plan, so he can expect nothing there.

Next he considers what he has for assets. How much will someone pay him for his car, TV, and all of the rest of his possessions? Matt does not own a home or a condo, but if he did, he would sell it too.

Matt calculates the total value of his assets, which is approximately $33,350. Sounds good, but Matt realizes he needs to pay off his debts before he goes anywhere! He has a car loan and he owes $5,000 on his credit cards. Matt also owes $3,500 in taxes.

Using the formula for net worth mentioned earlier, Sample 11 shows how much money Matt has for his five-year world trip.

SAMPLE 11
Matt's Net Worth

Assets	
Cash	$250
Emergency fund	1,500
Car	28,000
Vacation pay due	600
Assets	3,000
Total Assets	**$33,350**
Liabilities	
Car loan	$18,450
Credit cards	5,000
Taxes due	3,500
Total Liabilities	**$26,950**
Total Net Worth*	**$6,400**

* Formula: $33,350 (Assets) − $26,950 (Liabilities) = $6,400 (Net Worth)

Looks like Matt won't be running off to travel with *National Geographic* anytime soon. He has yet to calculate the costs of selling all of his possessions. His total net worth might last two months, if he is very careful. Matt decides he is better off continuing to pursue a career as a sommelier!

The surprising thing about your net worth is how quickly it can grow when you pay some attention to it. Consider Cassie: Last time we reviewed her affairs she had moved to her first apartment, was paying down her student loan of $20,000, and was looking forward to being debt-free. At that time her net worth statement was a negative number. Cassie continues to save money each and every month. Her student loan is almost paid off. By next year she anticipates her net worth statement will show a positive number.

By applying the funds she used to put aside for her emergency fund and student loans, Cassie is able to save toward her new goal of a deposit for a condo of her own. In the next three years she will have a positive net worth of $24,490! Let's take a look at Sample 12: Cassie's Net Worth Projection.

SAMPLE 12
Cassie's Net Worth Projection

	12 months after moving into her own apartment	24 months after moving into her own apartment	36 months after moving into her own apartment
Assets			
Cash	$600	$600	$600
Emergency fund	9,600	9,600	9,600
Pension plan	3,600	7,200	10,800
"Buy a condo" fund	0	1,750	3,490
Total Assets	**$13,800**	**$19,150**	**$24,490**
Liabilities			
Student loan	$13,500	$6,060	$0
Total Liabilities	**$13,500**	**$6,060**	**$0**
Total Net Worth	**$300**	**$13,090**	**$24,490**

2. Your Most Valuable Asset

Have you ever stopped to consider the value of your future earnings? After years of eating mac 'n' cheese as a student it can be hard to imagine yourself a wealthy person; however, the most valuable asset you have is *you*! Consider the following:

- You have *time*, meaning an entire lifetime ahead of you to reach your goals.

- You have *energy* — your 20s, 30s, and 40s are marked by a surge of energy. Many people put this energy toward their careers, making giant strides in just a few decades.

- You have *future income potential*. If you are in your mid-20s, you have approximately 40 career years ahead of you.

Do you know how much your earning potential is in the next 40 years? To provide you with a little perspective, let's take a look at Cassie, Matt, and Sam. How much money they will earn over their careers? (**Note:** I have used an inflation rate of 2 percent.)

Let's assume Cassie remains at her current work and that her income increases by inflation only. This is highly improbable as most young adults in their first career will see many changes in their work, and level of responsibilities, and their pay will increase accordingly. But even if Cassie were to never receive a promotion her lifetime, her income potential is more than $2 million! (Note that this does not take into consideration that Cassie's employer contributes to a pension plan for Cassie.) If Cassie stays with her employer until age 65, the value of her pension will be almost $900,000, or a lifetime income of $51,500 per year in retirement.

SAMPLE 13
Cassie's Lifetime Income Potential

Year	Age	Salary Income
2011	26	$36,000
2015	30	38,968
2020	35	43,023
2025	40	47,501
2030	45	52,445
2035	50	57,904
2040	55	63,930
2045	60	70,584
2050	**65**	**$2,096,539***

* This represents the accumulated total; all other figures preceding it reflect the annual income in the year.

Next let's take a look at Matt as he moves to his new career as a territory wine sales representative to the hospitality industry. He intends to work hard and smart. Matt plans to invest in his new career by furthering his education, taking courses in sales and programs specific to the hospitality industry. Doing so will lead to an increased pay scale and bonuses each year.

Within five years he expects to be making more than $60,000 a year. By the time Matt turns 37 he plans to become a sommelier. His income would then jump to $100,000 a year. If he works to age 65, Matt will have earned in excess of $5 million!

SAMPLE 14
Matt's Lifetime Income Potential

Year	Age	Base Salary + Bonus Income
2011	26	$45,000
2015	30	48,709
2020	35	71,706
2025	40	105,558
2030	45	116,545
2035	50	160,844
2040	55	177,584
2045	60	196,068
2050	65	$5,040,724*

* This represents the accumulated total; all other figures preceding it reflect the annual income in the year.

Sam's earnings in the first five years are suppressed because he's paying for the veterinary practice he has purchased from Dr. Wright. Once this loan is paid off, Sam's earnings are expected to rise to more than $100,000 per year. Since Sam is self-employed, he will need to save for his own retirement. However, with almost $6.5 million in total earnings this should be no problem for Sam. He recognizes that his veterinary practice is a valuable asset that he can sell when he is ready to retire.

SAMPLE 15
Sam's Lifetime Income Potential

Year	Age	Self-Employed Income
2011	26	$60,000
2015	30	100,000
2020	35	149,387
2025	40	164,935
2030	45	182,101
2035	50	201,055
2040	55	221,981
2045	60	245,085
2050	65	$6,401,207*

* This represents the accumulated total; all other figures preceding it reflect the annual income in the year.

3. Calculating Your Net Worth

Now that you understand how to calculate net worth, you may want to try it for yourself. Exercise 10 is included at the end of this section so you can calculate your own net worth. As you can see from the exercise it only goes to "Year 5." However, you can add more years to your own net worth statement. You may want to make it for ten years to help with your ten-year plan.

In Exercise 10, assets have been categorized as following:

- **Non-registered assets:** These are the amounts of money you have in savings, emergency fund, etc. Include money due to you from your employer, the tax man, and even from your family.

- **Tax-deferred accounts:** This refers to money that has been put away for either your retirement or educational funds for you or your children. Typically, these moneys are being saved for the long term (i.e., 10 to 20 years or more).

- **Lifestyle assets:** This refers to your possessions such as cars, boats, TVs, etc. Include the value you could expect to receive if you sold these items today, not the amount you paid, since possessions drop in value once they are used. If you own a home, condo, or cottage, record the value if you were to sell it in the next 90 days. If you are unsure how much this is, you may wish to ask a realtor for an opinion, or look online for homes similar to yours within your neighborhood which sold in the last year.

Once you have figured out all your assets, calculate the total.

Next you will record all of your liabilities. You may wish to call your lenders to request the current balance of your loans. Don't forget to include taxes you may owe. Total all of your liabilities.

Now subtract your total liabilities from your total assets. The amount remaining is your net worth.

Do not be discouraged if your first few years show a negative number; just keep working toward increasing your assets and reducing the size of your liabilities. I have watched clients who were able to increase their net worth from zero to hundreds of thousands of dollars in a few short years.

Keep your net worth statement updated. By reviewing and updating your statement every year, you will be able to take pride in watching your wealth grow.

Your up-to-date net worth statement is also an important tool in convincing lenders to lend you money for important expenditures such as buying a home or vehicle. This statement along with your cash flow statement shows you and the lenders that you are organized and in control of your finances.

In the next chapter, you will learn how to protect your net worth and your future income potential.

EXERCISE 10
Calculating Your Net Worth

Assets	Year 1	Year 2	Year 3	Year 4	Year 5
Non-Registered Assets					
Bank accounts					
Saving accounts					
GIC portfolio					
Mutual fund portfolio					
Investment portfolio					
Life insurance cash value					
Tax refund					
Vacation pay (due to you)					
Total Non-Registered Assets	$	$	$	$	$
Tax-Deferred Accounts					
Retirement savings					
Education savings					
Pension savings					
Total Tax-Deferred Accounts	$	$	$	$	$
Lifestyle Assets					
Vehicle					
Home					
Cottage					
Other (e.g., furniture, TV)					
Other					
Total Lifestyle Assets	$	$	$	$	$
Total Assets	$	$	$	$	$
Liabilities	Year 1	Year 2	Year 3	Year 4	Year 5
Vehicle loan					
Credit cards					
Rent or mortgage					
Personal line of credit					
Student loans					
Taxes you owe					
Total Liabilities	$	$	$	$	$
Total Net Worth	$	$	$	$	$

CHAPTER NINE

Create a Safety Net: Insurance

* Read this if you want to avoid unnecessary risk, and you want to know how to protect yourself.

* Read this if you place a high value on your growing net worth and future income potential.

* Read this if you need help understanding and selecting the right insurance policies.

Today, you likely own a vehicle, furnishings, and other possessions, which all have a value. Vehicle and property insurance are designed to protect your possessions. If you take a vacation, you will most likely buy travel insurance. You may have bought an extended warranty designed to replace your purchase of a faulty new laptop, TV, printer, or other products and appliances. If you have a pet, you can insure yourself against the cost of vet bills. But what about your life, health, and income replacement in the event you are ill or become disabled? Have you given any thought to the magnitude of the financial loss of your life or health?

Insurance is all about protecting what is most valuable and provides you with a safety net. Life is uncertain and none of us can see into the future; an insurance "safety net" will allow you to continue on your life's course with minimum interruptions when things go wrong.

1. Consider What You Should Insure

How do you decide what to insure? To answer that question, think about what you stand to lose and ask yourself the following questions:

- **Can I pay for the replacement of the insured item on my own?** In the case of your TV, computer, and other household items, or even the vet bills, the answer is yes. Though doing so might set you back a few months, this is not considered a catastrophic loss. However, if you have a skiing accident or become ill and lose one year or more of work, this is a catastrophe from which you may never fully recover.

- **What is the *most* I have to lose?** Here is where you measure the potential cost of your loss. If you hurt someone in a car accident, you could be sued for thousands or even millions of dollars. You might not be accustomed to thinking of yourself as an asset, but as you discovered in the previous chapter, *you* and your earning power are your biggest assets. During your lifetime, even if your income is modest, you will likely earn in excess of $2 million. As a professional or an executive, your earning potential could be in excess of $10 million.

- **Who will be affected by the loss?** When it comes to your assets or vacation plans, you are the one who will be affected by a loss. If you become ill, and cannot work, you are affected. When it comes to your vehicle, if you were to have an accident, you would be affected. The cost might be limited to repairing your car or someone else's car. However, if your passengers, the driver of another vehicle and/or his or her passengers, or even pedestrians were injured because of an accident you caused, many people could be affected. If you were to die, your spouse and children would be affected. The losses could run into millions of dollars.

1.1 Prioritize your insurance purchases

By now it should be clear to you that you insure the largest risk of loss first. The following is a list of what to insure in priority order.

1.1a Vehicle insurance

Vehicle insurance is first on the list because, in most areas, it's the law; and if you are in an at-fault accident (i.e., you hurt others and/or their property), you could be put in a position to be sued. Be sure to protect yourself with adequate liability coverage; one million dollars should be your minimum, but buy more if you can. Consider insuring your car for its replacement value; that way the amount your insurer covers will be equal to the cost of replacing your vehicle. Your coverage value should always be the same or higher than your outstanding loan.

A good driving record will help to keep your vehicle insurance rates low. Insurance rates vary widely based on your age, where you live, the value of the car, and the coverage purchased. Your insurance rates will change each year based on the characteristics listed. Vehicle insurance premiums vary widely, so shop around. Once you have identified a good insurance broker, he or she will help you to compare rates. One trick for keeping rates reduced is to increase your deductible (i.e., the amount you pay before making a claim).

1.1b Disability insurance

Disability is a risk no one should face without proper insurance coverage. As you have discovered, your income earning potential is your most valuable asset. There is a one in three chance of suffering at least one disability lasting more than 90 days before you reach the age of 65.[1] The following are two common sources of disability insurance:

- **Employee benefit plan:** Coverage may be offered through your employer's benefit package. If it is, make sure you sign up for the maximum available to you. Not only is this coverage low cost, by reviewing your employer's disability plan each year, you should be able to keep your level of coverage current with your income. Some employers and insurers put a cap on the maximum amount of monthly benefit. Take the time to understand your employers program to ensure you are properly protected. If your employer's plan pays less than 50 percent of your total pretax income, you may want to consider supplementing your employer's disability plan with an individual plan of your own.

- **Individual disability insurance policy:** If you are self-employed or your employer does not offer a disability plan, you will need to purchase an individual disability policy of your own. Whether you have disability insurance at work or not, it is a good idea to speak to a life-insurance advisor

---

[1] "Great-West Life 1985 Commissioner's Disability Table A," www.greatwestlife.com, accessed June 2011.

or a dual-licensed financial planner. Ask him or her to review your disability insurance options.

1.1c   Life insurance

If you are single, your need for life insurance is limited to having enough coverage to pay off your debts; add on another $10,000 to $15,000 for final expenses (e.g., funeral costs, taxes, and the legal and accounting costs to settle your estate). If you are single and your employer offers a benefit plan, you may have enough life insurance to meet your needs. Most employer plans will cover you for an amount equal to one year's income.

Life insurance is important when others depend on you. If you are married and/or have children, you will have a need for life insurance. In addition to the amount (above) for a single person, you will need to provide income replacement for your spouse and family. A simple guideline to follow is, cover yourself and your spouse for ten times as much as you earn in income each year (e.g., $45,000 [annual earnings] x 10 = $450,000). Again, whether you have life insurance at work or not, it is a good idea to speak to a life-insurance advisor or a dual-licensed financial planner. Ask him or her to review your life insurance options and make recommendations that suit your needs.

Keep your costs reduced by buying "term" insurance. Term insurance derives its name from the fact it is priced for a set period of "time" or "term" — typically the price will be set for ten years. You will be surprised at how affordable life insurance can be. One of my clients, a father of three children, told me the term life insurance I recommended was less expensive than the pet insurance he had been paying! He was embarrassed that he had been covering Lassie but had neglected to protect his family!

1.1d   Health insurance

If you are a resident of the United States, you will need to review your health insurance options with a professional, especially if your employer does not offer health insurance. Buying and keeping health insurance is an important part of financial security.

If you are a Canadian, the Canadian health-care system covers the cost of many serious illnesses and most of the basics. If your employer offers health and dental insurance, you are well protected. Since the Canadian system covers most catastrophic costs, the risk of an expensive loss is reduced. If your employer does not offer a health plan, you may wish to consider purchasing a health plan of your own. An individual health plan would cover the cost of prescriptions, ambulance services, semiprivate room, and other items not covered by the Canadian health-care plan.

1.1e Property insurance

If you rent an apartment, you may wish to protect your possessions with a fire and water damage insurance plan. Tenant's insurance will usually also protect you from theft. When you own a home of your own, you will purchase property insurance to protect your home or condo and its contents.

It is a good idea to keep a digital file with photos of your possessions as well as copies for your invoices. You may want to send a copy to your insurer. Similar to your vehicle insurance, it is a good idea to purchase replacement insurance. That way if your five-year old sofa is destroyed, your insurer will provide you with enough money to purchase a new sofa, *not* a five-year old sofa! Property insurance usually pays for your accommodation while your home is uninhabitable, in addition to any cleanup costs.

1.1f Critical illness insurance

Critical illness insurance pays out a lump sum in the event you are diagnosed with one of the critical illnesses named in the policy assuming you are still living (usually 30- to 60-day waiting period) after diagnosis. Cancer, heart disease, and stroke are the most commonly covered illnesses.

This type of coverage can be useful for those who are unable to acquire disability insurance or who wish to have a lump sum to pay for debt or other costs in the event they become seriously ill.

Speak to a licensed insurance advisor for more information. Some employers now include critical illness insurance in their benefits packages.

1.1g Travel insurance

Travel insurance is usually purchased through your travel agent. This coverage will pay for the cost of canceling your vacation in the event you are too ill to travel and your doctor confirms this with your insurer. It will also help you to return home in the event of an out-of-country emergency.

By all means, consider travel insurance when you are booking your vacation well in advance. If you are traveling last minute, ask yourself, how much might a return flight and other associated costs be? Check with your employer's health plan; you may be covered while out of the country. If you are, confirm that your days of coverage exceed the days you will be out of the country.

1.1h Other insurance

By now, you have likely figured out that the biggest risks you face in life have nothing to do with your widescreen TV or your pet's vet bills. Some of these coverages seem borderline nonsensical. For example, I was recently offered an extended warranty for a printer I purchased for $100. The cost of the extended warranty was $50! That is 50 percent of the cost to insure an item I can easily afford to replace. Yet it is all too easy to add the cost of product insurance to your charge card as you are standing in the store with an eager salesperson, while all you want to do is get home to enjoy your purchase.

2. Learn by Example

Matt spends several thousands of dollars each year on car insurance. He does so because he sees his car as his single largest asset. He wants to protect himself from the cost associated with repairing or replacing his car in the event of an accident. His car insurance also protects him from liability in the event he hurts others, their property, or causes damage to another vehicle. These are all good reasons to make his monthly car insurance premium.

What about Matt's most valuable asset? In Chapter 8, you discovered that Matt's income potential is in excess of $5 million. When Matt told Cassie about his broken ankle he expected some sympathy, but instead Cassie seemed annoyed. Matt asked her about her reaction.

Cassie explained to Matt that she keeps an emergency fund so she can meet her financial obligations even if she is ill, hurt, or loses her job. In the event of an illness lasting longer than 90 days, Cassie has a disability insurance policy that will replace 70 percent of her income while she is unable to work.

Cassie asked Matt, "What is worth more to you, your car or your future income? What if you had hurt your back, who would look after you and pay your expenses while recovering? How long could you live on your credit cards?" Clearly Cassie was not impressed. She explained to Matt that insuring his income is equally important to insuring his car and most likely would cost no more than his vehicle insurance.

After price-checking with a few different insurance agents, Matt discovered that a disability insurance policy would cost approximately $1,200 a year, and his premiums would be guaranteed not to change until he turns 65.

If you are self-employed like Sam is, you must be prepared to provide for yourself and protect yourself from loss.

Sam interviews three insurance advisors who are experts in disability insurance. He selects a life and health insurance advisor who has also earned her Certified Financial Planner (CFP) designation. Sam's advisor will be able to work with him to create a comprehensive financial plan. By working with a qualified life and health insurance advisor, Sam is able to put a comprehensive program in place. He purchases disability insurance. Sam's future income potential is in excess of $6 million; therefore, protecting his income must be his first priority. He is comforted to know that his income will continue during periods of illness or disability.

Sam's insurance advisor explains to him that as his advisor and financial planner, her role is a six-step process to help Sam determine what is best for him:

1. Research available disability plans and who offers them. This will include a review of coverage available through professional associations and government plans.

2. Explain to Sam the features and benefits of the differing contracts.

3. Help Sam to articulate what is most important to him and what his largest concerns are. Sam's advisor discovers that Sam is most concerned about having as much protection as possible, and Sam is frugal and does not like wasting money.

4. Choose a payment start date and maximum payment period. Sam tells his advisor he could wait up to 120 days before benefits begin, but if he is disabled he wants his payments to continue as long as he is unable to work. Sam's advisor suggests a 90-day waiting period. That way his first disability payment will arrive 30 days later with benefits extending to age 65 or until Sam would be well enough to return to work.

5. Sam's advisor then prepares a comparison from the top three insurers, offering Sam the coverage he requested.

6. Finally, Sam's advisor helps him to make a final selection, complete the paperwork, and arrange for the necessary medical exams. Once the policy is issued, Sam's advisor will review his coverage with him to make sure everything is in order.

Sam's insurance advisor tells him the benefits of owning a disability policy of his own:

- The only person who can cancel the policy is Sam. A noncancelable policy means the insurer cannot cancel or change Sam's policy once it is issued, even if Sam were to become seriously ill.

- Premiums are guaranteed by the insurer not to change from the time of purchase until Sam reaches age 65.

- Sam can choose from several options:

  - Cost of living increases during disability so his income keeps up with inflation.

  - Sam can increase his coverage over time with a Future Earnings Protection Option (FEPO) as his income increases and without having to prove his good health.

  - The regular occupation option provides Sam protection from having to take on work which is less desirable than his qualifications entitle him to.

  - The refund of premium refunds 50 percent of Sam's premiums every seven years if he does not make any claims.

Based on Sam's interview with his advisor, Sam chooses a noncancelable plan with guaranteed premiums to age 65. Sam will receive $4,500 a month starting 90 days after he becomes disabled.

The optional benefits he chose are the future earnings protection and the cost of living benefit. Since he does not like to waste money, Sam likes the refund of premium benefit because he gets 50 percent of his premiums refunded to him every seven years if he remains healthy.

If Sam took advantage of all of the above benefits and options, he expects his premiums to be approximately $2,500 a year. Assuming Sam was lucky enough to never make a claim and he kept his policy to age 65, his total premiums would be $100,000 and his insurer would refund him 50 percent or $50,000. Over his lifetime it would cost Sam $50,000 to protect the $6 million he expects to earn by age 65.

If Sam is less than lucky, and suffers from a long-term disability, Sam's policy will provide him with more than peace of mind; it will provide him with much needed income — a safety net for uncertain times.

Sam is now ready to review his health insurance needs. His advisor suggests that as a small-business owner they should review options for an individual health insurance plan.

Sam feels good about his choice since he now knows what his options are and which benefits and features are most important to him. He is happy with his advisor since she answered all of his questions and took the time to help him choose the best plans for his needs. As a CFP, Sam's financial planner will be there for him as he grows his practice, ready to help Sam build a strategic and comprehensive plan to achieve his financial goals, and protect him against potential loss.

3. A Typical Employer's Benefit Plan

Benefits are only as valuable as your ability to take advantage of them. Start by knowing what is available to you. If you have an employee benefit plan, you may need to supplement it with additional insurance. Become familiar with your employer's insurance offerings and the options you can make, if any. This way you will know what additional insurance you will need.

If you do not have an employee handbook, ask for one. In your employee handbook, here is what you might expect to find:

- **Life insurance:** Most employer plans will offer at least a small amount of life insurance. Typical amounts of coverage are either a fixed amount (e.g., $25,000 to $50,000) or a multiple of your annual income. Some employers' benefit plans will allow you to increase your coverage by making an application.

- **Accident, disability, and dismemberment insurance:** Most employer plans include this coverage. The amount is typically the same as your basic life insurance. To qualify for a payment, your death would have to be the result of an accident. If your family needs life insurance, they will need it regardless of the cause of your death so make sure you get additional coverage.

- **Short-term disability insurance:** Some employer plans cover a short-term illness or disability, typically starting after seven days and lasting 120 days. If you qualify, you can expect to receive anywhere from 50 to 100 percent of your salary while you are unable to work due to an illness or disability. Check your employee handbook to determine your level of coverage. If your employer offers this coverage, count yourself among the lucky few.

- **Long-term disability insurance:** This is the biggie, and not all employer plans offer long-term disability insurance. This coverage provides income replacement while you are off work due to an illness or disability lasting more than 120 days. Check your plan to see how long payments will continue. Some plans offer a two-year or a five-year benefit, while others will provide income replacement until age 65 or until you recover. The amount of income can vary widely from 50 to 75 percent of your income. Some plans have a maximum monthly payment; common maximums are $2,500 and $5,000 a month. If your employer's coverage is less than 50 percent of your total pretax income, consider purchasing a personal disability policy of your own. If your employer does not offer long-term disability insurance, it is important that you buy coverage of your own.

- **Health insurance:** Most employer plans will offer some health coverage. These plans normally provide coverage for both catastrophic events and the more mundane health issues such as paramedical (i.e., chiropractic, massage, and physiotherapy) services and prescription drugs.

- **Dental insurance:** Dental insurance is a misnomer, since dental plans are designed by insurers to be self-paying. If your employer offers a dental plan, no matter how meager, thank them. If you are in a position to choose between benefits for yourself, I strongly recommend you leave the dental benefits to the last, since they offer the least amount of insurance protection and the cost of dental is easily predicted. Instead, use your benefit dollars to increase, in this order, your long- and short-term disability coverage, your health benefits, and life insurance if you have a family.

4. Tips for Choosing an Insurance Provider

Before selecting an insurance agent it is important to understand the distinction between a *life* and *health* insurance agent and a *property* insurance agent. The life and health insurance agent protects *lives* and provides coverage to protect you and your family in the event you die, have an accident, or are too ill to work. The property insurance agent protects *things*. He or she will provide you with coverage for your vehicle, apartment, etc. Generally the person who provides life and health insurance does not provide coverage for your possessions.

Choose insurance advisors for your life and property you trust and who are prepared to demonstrate the value of their recommendations. Your advisor is there to help you select the insurer who is financially sound and able to meet his or her commitments. Only buy insurance from the most financially sound insurance companies.

This is one area where, if it sounds too good to be true, it probably is. The following are some additional tips:

- Get a referral from your friends, family, or peers by asking who they use and if they would recommend this person.

- Avoid anyone who sells insurance as a sideline. Providing insurance advice requires dedication to the industry, clients, and continuing education.

- Determine if your advisor has any professional designations and what they are. There are many professional designations, so ask about the advisor's qualifications and the meaning of the designations he or she holds.

- Most importantly, interview several advisors to determine how comfortable you are with them. Do they seem to be genuinely interested in you and your goals?

Check the following websites to see if the advisor you are interviewing is a member in good standing:

- United States: National Association of Insurance and Financial Advisors (NAIFA), www.naifa.org

- Canada: Advocis (Financial Advisors Association of Canada), www.advocis.ca

If he or she is not a member of either NAIFA or Advocis, ask about associations with which he or she is affiliated.

The most important tip when buying insurance of any kind is to remember you are paying a small premium to protect yourself from loss. The insurer is on the hook to make a large payout to you in the event of a catastrophe. Trust is all-important. Choose an advisor you trust and who is prepared to demonstrate the value of his or her recommendations. Your advisor is there to help you select the insurer who is financially sound and able to meet its commitments. Only buy insurance from the most financially sound insurance company.

4.1 Life and health insurance advisor

Your life and health insurance advisor is well-qualified to help you select the health, disability, and life insurance that is right for you using the six-step process as outlined by Sam's insurance advisor. Many life and health insurance agents have advanced training in financial planning and will work with you to create a financial plan to reach your insurance, savings, and investment goals.

This advisor provides expert advice on and offers health, life, and disability insurance as well as savings products from guaranteed investment certificates (GIC) to mutual funds. Since new graduates and early stage career developers have a need for health and disability insurance products, insurance agents are happy to work with you. Many have their certified financial planner (CFP) designation and are happy to prepare a comprehensive financial plan providing advice on both insurance and investments as part of their service.

4.2 Property insurance advisor

Now that you have taken care of your most valuable asset — *you* — it is time to provide coverage for your home and vehicle. Using the tips in section **4.** you should be able to identify a property insurer who can provide you with quality care and coverage for your valuable possessions. In addition to speaking to friends and family about who they enjoy working with to protect their property, check your local phone book for listings of home and vehicle insurance agents. Interview several and choose the person with whom you are most comfortable. Do not select a property insurance advisor or insurer based on price alone. Prices may vary widely, but so too may the level of coverage and service.

Here are some additional tips when you buying property insurance:

- Ask for replacement coverage whenever possible. The cost is a few pennies more, but the benefits can be huge.

- Buy enough coverage to meet your needs; do not underinsure.

- Liability insurance: In the event you are sued, it pays to have as much as possible. One million dollars should be your bare minimum; ideally buy $2 million or more.

- Save money on your insurance premiums by increasing the deductible. The deductible is the amount you pay out of your own pocket before being able to make a claim, therefore reducing the risk to the insurer, meaning your insurer will reduce premiums.

CHAPTER TEN

Debt

* Read this chapter if you want to use debt prudently.

* Read this chapter if you want to know what you should do to protect yourself from your creditors. (**Note:** The terms "lender" and "creditor" in this chapter are interchangeable.)

It may seem as if "debt" is a four-letter word of the caliber we do not say out loud in polite company, but the truth is much more complicated than that.

Debt has its uses and if used properly, can increase your wealth at a much faster rate than if you tried to pay cash for everything. Just imagine that you lived in a country where the citizens could not borrow to buy a home. You along with your friends, family, and neighbors would be forced to save money until you could purchase your home with cash. With the average price of a home at two-and-a-half to four times your annual gross income, it might take your entire lifetime to save enough money to buy a home. In the meantime, you might be forced to live with your parents while you save as much money as possible. If you had to pay rent while saving to pay cash for a home, you might never reach your goal. Yet historically a home has provided the average person with their most valuable asset. This asset can then be sold in later years to create retirement income.

1. The Difference between Good Debt and Bad Debt

Clearly debt has its place in our society, but how do you distinguish between good debt and bad debt?

Good debt allows you, the borrower, to increase your wealth by —

- funding your educational costs and leading to a career in which your earnings are higher than they would have been otherwise;

- financing a vehicle purchase allowing you to commute to your job;

- taking on a mortgage to purchase a home, which will retain its value and grow in value over time; and

- borrowing to invest or to start a business which leads to increased earnings.

You can spot bad debt very easily. Bad debt does *not* grow your wealth. Instead, it reduces your wealth because the cost of servicing the debt takes away from your ability to save money. Examples of bad debt include:

- Carrying debt on your credit card. If you charged a pair of jeans or video game on your department store or charge card and it stays on your card past the next statement, this is an example of bad debt.

- Charging for meals when dining out, lattes, and other *wants* but not *needs* are other examples of bad debt.

- Borrowing to purchase appliances, furniture, TVs, etc. Many furniture retailers offer one- or two-year, no payment, interest-free loans on purchases. Be aware, however, that shoppers who pay cash are usually able to negotiate a discount for doing so. Personally, I can think of few things less pleasant than paying for a used sofa, even if it is my used sofa. Yet many people do this every single year. Worse, they do not pay the balance off at the end of the two years of free interest, but rather, begin to make payments for the next one to three years at interest rates that are frequently in excess of 20 percent. By the time you have it paid off, you are ready for a new sofa!

2. Understand What Your Lender Is Saying

Your lender speaks the language of interest rates. The rate of interest your lender charges reflects the level of perceived risk. The higher the risk the more the lender charges.

Before you are able to borrow, your lender will need to know your credit score. If you have a poor credit rating, expect to pay a higher rate than your friends who have a high credit score. The high interest rate your lender charges you may mean the lender thinks of you as a credit risk and that your purchasing decisions may be poor. Since you will need to prove your credit worthiness, you too should become familiar with your credit score. Contact Equifax or TransUnion to find out your credit score.

Let's take a look at some typical interest rates currently charged by lenders for a variety of items:

- Mortgage on your home: 3 to 6.5 percent[1]

- Student loans: 5 percent or more[2]

- Line of credit (car): 5 to 8 percent

- Low-interest credit card: 9 percent

- Standard credit card: 18 percent

- Department store credit card: 23 percent or more

By looking at the list, it is clear that lenders think most highly of borrowers when they are borrowing for an asset such as a home. Borrowing for a big screen TV, a pair of jeans, or a meal at an expensive restaurant is rightly seen by your lender as an example of poor judgment on your part, one you will be punished for by paying a high interest rate.

3. Helpful Credit Tips

Now that you know the difference between good debt and bad debt and you know what your lenders are charging, which debts do you plan to pay off first? It only makes sense to first pay off loans with the highest interest rates.

---

[1] Canada Mortgage, "Rates," www.canadamortgage.com/ratesshow/showrates.cfm, (2011), accessed June 2011.

[2] CBS, "Money Watch," www.moneywatch.bnet.com, (2011), accessed June 2011.

Before you make a purchase on your charge card or borrow to buy consumer goods, think about whether or not you really need the item. What is the useful life of your purchase? Match the term of the loan to the useful lifetime of the item being purchased. To quote Dr. Joyce Brothers, "Credit buying is much like being drunk. The buzz happens immediately and gives you a lift. The hangover comes the day after."

The following tips will help keep you out of trouble:

- **30-day debt:** You should pay your credit card balance in full when your statement arrives. If you are buying a pair of jeans on your charge card, pay off your credit card balance at the end of each month. Always pay cash for lattes, which are consumed moments after you pay for them.

- **1- to 2-year debt:** Arrange for a line of credit with your bank. If you are buying a computer and plan to use it for two to three years, your loan repayment period should not exceed two years. If you are buying furniture or appliances and you do not have cash but want to take advantage of those retailers who offer a one- to two-year, no payment, interest-free loan, make plans to pay the balance off in full at the end of the interest-free period.

- **2- to 5-year debt:** The typical term for a vehicle loan is between two to five years. If you are borrowing to buy a vehicle, plan to keep it for five to ten years. Never borrow for a vehicle where you are required to make a bubble payment at the end since you could easily find yourself at the end of the loan paying more than the vehicle is worth! Worse, if you do not have cash, you may be forced to borrow once again to pay the remaining balance.

- **5- to 25-year debt:** Be careful not to overextend yourself with student loan debt. Your student debt level should never exceed your potential future earnings. A good rule of thumb is your debt should not exceed half of your expected yearly earnings. If your expected pretax earnings are $40,000, your debt level should not exceed $20,000. Even at these levels it will take you many years to repay this loan. A comfortable loan payment for new graduates is generally believed to be 5 percent of income. Given the example, the new graduate earning $40,000 a year with $20,000 of debt can afford to pay

$166 a month. Assuming three differing interest rates, the following list shows how long it will take to pay off that loan:

- Interest rate of 8 percent: it will take 20 years to pay off a $20,000 student loan.

- Interest rate of 6 percent: it will take 15 years to pay off a $20,000 student loan.

- Interest rate of 4 percent: it will take 13 years to pay off a $20,000 student loan.

Remember that student debt in both Canada and the US is not easy to walk away from because it generally doesn't qualify for bankruptcy protection. It is a good idea to pay off your student loans as quickly as possible. Is it any wonder graduating students are fleeing back to the family home? If you are one of these graduates, make good use of your time at home by reducing your debt as soon as possible — pay as much in debt payments as it would cost you to rent an apartment.

- **25 years:** Borrowing to buy a home. Traditionally a lender's favorite since the perceived risk is the lowest. If you default on the mortgage payments, your lender can sell your home to recoup its losses. A typical mortgage will be amortized over 25 years. The typical home may be expected to last 50 years or more and to grow in value over time. The wealthiest people I have met during my years as a financial planner typically paid off their mortgages in 15 years or less. Once they did, they continued to save the same amount of dollars previously spent on their mortgage to their retirement nest egg.

4. What to Do When Things Go Wrong

The frightening news is more and more young adults are beginning life with a significant amount of debt. Research from the Financial Consumer Agency of Canada confirms:

- 60 percent of young adults age 18 to 29 carry some debt.

- 35 percent have debt levels exceeding $10,000.

- 21 percent have debt of $20,000 or more.

- 40 percent admit to not having enough funds to cover monthly expenses at least once during the prior year.

So you have some debt and, after reading this, you decide you want to do something about it. Will that student loan ever be paid off? How did your credit card balances get so high? Maybe you do not have a budget or, if you do, you have not been paying attention to it. Now is the time to resolve to take back control of your debt. If you only make the minimum payment each month, you will be paying for that pair of jeans for many years to come. If you recall the example from the introduction, the $60 you spent on jeans will cost you in excess of $325. How long will you be wearing those jeans?

To regain control:

- Review your budget.
- Reduce spending for "wants."
- Pay off the loans with the highest interest rate first.
- Stop using your charge cards until you have them paid off.
- Save for other goals. Reallocate a part of your savings budget towards reducing your debt. Resume savings after your charge cards are paid off. (Remember to keep an emergency fund.)
- Double or triple your credit card payments. If you lack the discipline, ask your bank to automatically transfer a specified amount each month to your debt.
- Commit to paying cash for all future nonessential purchases.

If you find you are having trouble making your payments on time due to job loss or low savings, have a frank discussion with your creditors before you default on your landlord, your loans, or your credit card payments. Tell them about your situation and ask for their patience. It is always good advice to act promptly when your lender contacts you. Book an appointment to review your case. Ask lots of questions to ensure you understand everything that is being said and what is being offered. If you are granted a loan modification, ask for the conditions and have it put in writing.

One solution is to negotiate a loan consolidation. This means your loans are bundled into a single loan. This is a good idea when —

- the new interest rate being charged is *less* than the current average rate you are now paying, and
- your total monthly payment is *lower* than your current payment.

If you are still having difficulty, you may wish to contact a credit counselor who will help you to renegotiate your loans.

The consequences of not making your loan payments in a timely manner include:

- Loss of your good credit score. This will make it difficult to borrow in the future and will mean your lender will ask for higher interest rates on the loan as he or she rightfully sees you as a high risk.

- Added costs as your lenders will tack on late fees and interest to your existing debt.

- If you have failed to pay an outstanding bill, your account may be filed with a collection agency whose job is to collect what is owed. A collection agency can be very aggressive about collecting what is owed, causing you embarrassment and additional charges.

- In a final push to get paid, your creditors may file an order with the court for the money you owe them. If the court grants the judgment, your employer will be instructed to reduce (i.e., garnish) your wages by the amount owing to satisfy your creditor.

- If you are finding it impossible to meet your financial obligations, you may have to file for bankruptcy. This will help you to avoid your creditors, but it also means that you will not be able to borrow or use a charge card for many years — usually seven years.

Debt is like whipping cream — a little goes a long way and its volume can unexpectedly increase dramatically. When you fail to make timely payments toward your loans, you may find yourself in a position where fees and interest charges are added to your loan balances. If you are having problems with debt, the following government websites offer excellent advice:

- United States Federal Trade Commission: www.ftc.gov

- Financial Consumer Agency of Canada: www.fcac-acfc.gc.ca

Both websites offer tips for negotiating your current debts and information on finding reputable credit counseling agencies that can help you.

Clearly, having problems with debt is to be avoided. Your best defence is to live within your means and keep an emergency fund to carry you through the bad times. Doing so will help you to appreciate the advantages of good debt and you will never have to think of debt as a naughty four-letter word!

CHAPTER ELEVEN

Saving and Investing

* Read this if you want to know how to invest your savings.

Your 20s is a time when you strive to reach a variety of short-term goals. Many of these goals will be "firsts" such as a first vacation, first car, first apartment, and first home. At this time in your life it is a good idea to allocate 80 percent of your savings to your short-term goals, investing the remaining 20 percent to your long-term goals. For example, if you are saving $100 a month, $80 may be put aside for your emergency fund, savings for a vacation, or deposit for a vehicle or home purchase. The other $20 should be invested for the long term.

Saving is the act of putting money aside for a future date or expense. When you were a child, you likely kept your savings in a piggy bank. Your grandparents may have kept their savings under their mattress. A better place to keep your savings is in a savings account which provides safety from loss and pays you interest. Savings accounts, Certificates of Deposit, and Guaranteed Investment Certificates (GICs) are a good place to keep the money you will need to spend in the next few years. In the event that your financial institution fails, Federal Deposit Insurance Corporation (FDIC) in the US and Canada Deposit Insurance Corporation (CDIC) will work for you by insuring your savings and offering protection against loss of deposits.

Investing is the process of putting your money (also called capital) to work in order to gain profitable returns; this could be in the form of interest, dividend, income, or appreciation in capital value. If you have money that you do not plan to spend in the next five to ten years or more, you may consider investing it. Traditional investments include mutual funds, stocks, and bonds.

The key message of this chapter is: The best way to grow your wealth is by saving a little of your income each and every time you get paid. Set your savings program on autopilot, transferring money directly to saving accounts for each goal every month. One day you will look back and be able to see what you have accomplished with a few dollars a day.

1. The Four Principles for Building Your Foundation of Wealth

The wealthy person saves money to purchase assets that create income so that working for a living becomes optional. How does the average person become wealthy? By following the principles described in the next four sections.

1.1 Debt control

Now is the time to get debt under control. You may recall the formula for net worth is *assets - liabilities = net worth*. Net worth is the key measurement of wealth. Not only does debt detract from your net worth, the cost of servicing your debt each month reduces the amount of money left over for savings. Try this, once you pay off a loan; continue to deposit the same amount into one of your savings or investment accounts. Instead of paying your lender, you will now pay yourself! By reducing your debt and growing your savings, you will become wealthy.

1.2 Delayed gratification

You might ask yourself: "What good does it do to save a few dollars a day?" Even very small contributions add up over time. Remember Cassie's budget plans? By skipping a daily latte on the way to work she saves $4 a day. By adding one more dollar a day, she is able to invest $150 a month. Knowing that the cost of her coffee will go up each year, Cassie is able to increase her savings to keep up with an inflation rate of 2 percent. Assuming Cassie invests her $5 a day savings in the TSX index, her investment earns 10 percent annually.[1] The value of Cassie's investment would look like the following:

- Year 10 = $32,000

- Year 20 = $125,000

- Year 30 = $372,000

- Year 40 = Her portfolio would be worth more than $1,000,000

The following graph shows the results. Contributions are represented in the bars at the bottom. The value of her portfolio is shown in the sweeping upward line. Because Cassie makes a small sacrifice of a daily coffee, her investments are multiplying faster than a pair of pet hamsters!

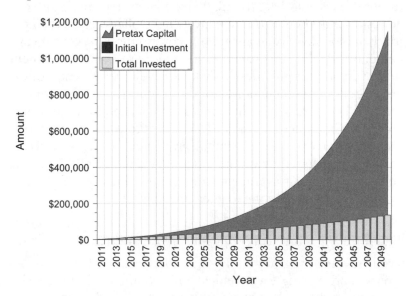

---

[1] MoneySense, "Classic Couch Potato Portfolio: Historical performance tables," www.moneysense.ca/2006/04/05/classic-couch-potato-portfolio-historical-performance-tables, (2006), accessed June 2011.

Note: The graph's rate of return assumptions show what would happen if your contributions earned a similar return to the Canadian stock market (TSX) from 1976 to 2009. The effects of taxation have been ignored.

1.3 Diversification

When making an investment decision, investors hope for the perfect blend of high return and low risk. This perfect investment does not exist. In fact, the opposite holds true; the higher the return, the higher the risk.

By investing in a wide variety of assets you may be said to have a "diversified" portfolio. The beauty of diversification is that it reduces the risk of the loss of your capital by spreading that risk over a wide variety of assets. As you begin to save and invest, consider diversification to be your best friend. The largest pension funds and money managers in North America use the principal of diversification to protect and grow the investments they manage for their clients. You should too.

1.4 Dollar cost averaging

If diversification is your best friend, then dollar cost averaging is your second best friend when it comes to investing. Dollar cost averaging is the principal of making regular monthly contributions to your investment accounts. Adding a constant dollar amount to your investment each and every month provides you with a lower overall cost. For example, you add a $100 each month to your mutual fund. More mutual fund units will be purchased when prices are low, and fewer units will be purchased when prices are high. The benefit to you is a lower total average *cost per share* of the investment, giving you a lower overall cost for the shares purchased over time. As a secondary benefit, investors who follow a dollar cost averaging strategy have a discipline in place that prevents them from trying to guess the market.

2. Priorities for Your Savings and Investments

Start your savings program with your short-term goals such as an emergency fund. Saving for a vehicle and a home could be considered your mid-term goals. Once you have established savings plans for the things you want to accomplish in the next few years, set aside a few dollars for your long-term goals.

The primary objective when saving for your short-term goals is the safety of your capital from risk of loss and the ability to access your funds quickly. When investing for your long-term goals, invest for growth at a reasonable risk. Take your time and learn all you can about the investments that interest you. Practice the principals of dollar cost averaging and diversification by investing regularly in a good quality mutual fund.

2.1 Priority 1: Emergency fund

An emergency fund should be your first savings goal. If you recall in Chapter 5, as Cassie planned to leave the family home and get an apartment of her own, her parents insisted she save enough for the deposit on her apartment and an emergency fund.

You may have heard that you should save six to nine months of your annual income in case of an emergency. An emergency fund is an important part of your financial security. Having money put aside in case of job loss or an unexpected expense such as a major vehicle repair or medical emergency, is good advice. But how do you save more than half of your yearly income? Most people simply do not have the discretionary income to save half or even a quarter of their income. If you are still living with your parents, now is the time when it is possible to save six months of income for an emergency.

For those of you who are already living on your own and have financial obligations, a more realistic goal would be to save one to three months of income. If you save 10 percent of your monthly income each month you will have an emergency fund equal to one month's pay at the end of the year. If this is too hard, try saving 5 percent and it will take you two years to save the equivalent of one month's pay.

The more secure your employment, the less of an emergency fund you will need. The opposite is also true, if your employment is at risk, or you are self-employed, the larger your emergency fund should be.

Since you may need to access this money on short notice, the only safe place for your emergency fund is in a high-interest savings account. Check with your bank or credit union's offerings for the best daily interest rate. A high-interest savings account may not offer an exciting rate of return, but it does offer you security of capital and quick access to your funds.

2.2 Priority 2: Where you should invest your savings for mid-term goals

Mid-term goals include the savings you are putting aside for a vehicle or deposit on a home you plan to purchase in the next two to five years. Start by placing the money you are saving towards your future goals in a high-interest savings account. Each time you have $1,000 in your savings account consider buying a Guaranteed Investment Certificates (GIC) and Certificates of Deposit (CD), which mature shortly before your planned purchase. For example, you're saving $400 a month and plan to buy your car in 24 months. After the third month you will have saved $1,200; you move this money to a GIC or CD that matures in 18 to 20 months. Three months later you have saved another $1,200 and you move these funds to a GIC or CD that matures in 15 to 18 months. Keep doing this until you are ready to buy your car. GICs and CDs offer a higher interest rate than a savings account, and your money is safe. Typically your bank-held savings are protected by insurance.

Note that GICs and CDs are purchased for a set period of time and pay a guaranteed rate of interest. You may not be able to access you funds until the maturity date.

2.3 Priority 3: Investing for long-term goals

You have your short-term and mid-term goals set up. You are making regular contributions towards your savings. Now you find yourself with a little extra savings each month that you can put towards your long-term goals. These savings can be invested.

Maybe your employer offers a retirement savings plan. Many employers offer to match your savings with company dollars when you join the company retirement savings plan. Short of folding your money in half, this is the fastest way to double it!

Maybe you want to take advantage of tax savings by making deposits to a registered retirement account. It is possible to begin investing in a well-diversified mutual fund with as little as a $50-deposit and future contributions of $25.

You may be a little nervous and excited about investing your money. After all, investing is saving's sexy cousin. You watch TV and some announcer is screaming at you about this opportunity or other: "Buy gold! Sell oil!" You ask yourself, "How do I get in on the action?" My advice is to take it slow. You want to *invest* your savings, not *gamble* them away. Investing requires discipline, patience, and wisdom — think Warren Buffett, not some screaming talking head trying to increase his or her TV ratings.

Let's review the definition of investing: Investing is the process of putting your money to work in order to gain profitable returns; this could be in the form of interest, dividends, or appreciation in capital value.

The money you do not plan to spend in the next seven to ten years or more may be invested. Since you will not need to access these funds for many years, there is a wide variety of investment vehicles available, from mutual funds to stocks and bonds.

The key attribute of investing is that your money is working for you to earn a profit. Money you invest in mutual funds or the stock market differs from the money in your savings accounts. Mutual funds and the stock market offer a *potential* for a higher return on your capital, but this potential comes with risk. Unlike your savings accounts, returns are not guaranteed and your balance may fluctuate dramatically over time.

The best way to start your investing experience is with mutual funds. A mutual fund is a professionally managed type of collective investment that pools money from many investors. Investments are professionally managed. The fund manager strives to grow the portfolio by investing in a diversified basket of stocks, bonds, and money market instruments or other securities.

Mutual funds offer the following advantages to beginning investors:

- You can open an investment account with a very small initial deposit.

- You can make small regular deposits.

- Your money is managed by a professional money manager.

- Diversification provides a reduction in risk of loss by spreading the risk over a wide variety of assets. Ownership in a mutual fund means you will have access to and own a portion of many national and international corporations which you could not do on your own.

- Because you can purchase mutual funds for small monthly contributions, you can take advantage of dollar cost averaging and put your money to work right away.

This means that once you have chosen the mutual fund that meets your goals, you will not have to make day-to-day investment decisions of your own.

3. Talk to a Financial Planner

Speak to a financial planner before investing your money. Choosing investments can be very confusing. A financial planner will help you to understand the available choices and assist you in making the right decision for you. He or she will ask you several questions in order to better understand your investment goals and risk tolerance. Here is a sample of the questions you should ask yourself before making an investment decision:

- When will I need to access these funds?

- What rate of return do I expect to earn on my investments?

- Is that rate of return realistic?

- Am I most interested in the maximum growth of my investment?

- Am I more interested in the safety of my capital?

- How will I feel if my investment loses money?

Your financial planner will make a few recommendations. Before you make a final selection, ask the financial planner the following questions:

- How does your recommendation meet my goals?

- Has the fund been available for ten years or more? Funds with a long track history have demonstrated their ability over time.

- Would you (the financial planner) consider this fund to be a "core" holding? It is advisable to choose a core fund with a long track history. Core holdings are the meat and potatoes of investing. They should form the core or bulk of every portfolio. Leave the exotic funds to more experienced investors. Sector or speculative funds are like a double chocolate truffle — eat too many and you will end up with a tummy ache!

- Who is the fund manager? How long has he or she been managing this fund?

- How has this investment performed in the past?

- Is it realistic to expect the same performance in the future?

- How volatile is this fund? How much did the fund gain in its best year, and lose in its worst year?

- What are the risks involved in buying this fund?

- What are the fees associated with this fund?

A good fund manager can achieve above-average results. When choosing between two funds with a similar mandate and historical return, choose the one with the lowest volatility (beta) and the lowest fees.

Be cautious. Funds with the highest return last year may be this year's worst performing funds. Remember you are investing to achieve a profit. Investing does not mean gambling.

Keep the four principals of your foundation of wealth in mind as you make saving and investment decisions and review your account and progress with your financial planner at least once a year.

4. Know Your Money Style and Avoid the Pitfalls

There are few relationships more complicated than the one you will have with your money. Some people are intimate with every detail of their finances — endlessly doing research and keeping track of every penny. Others are more distant and have a general knowledge of how money is being utilized, but they are not sure if they are doing enough to meet their goals. They may only be comfortable saving their money when the rate of return is guaranteed. Then there are the emotional types who make impulsive decisions resulting in buying and selling at the wrong times.

Different investors have different attitudes towards finances. Which group best describes you?

- **Geek Investor:** You're great at budgeting and analyzing data, but don't know when to stop researching and start acting.

- **Cautious Investor:** You have a grasp of your finances. You avoid risks. Although you have goals, you could use help planning your investments to better meet your goals.

- **Emotional Investor:** You always keep your immediate individual needs in mind when making financial decisions, but are prone to making impulsive choices, forsaking long-term needs.

So, what kind of investor are you? Not sure? Take Quiz 2 and identify your investment style. This can help you to figure out where your strategy is most vulnerable to pitfalls or problems.

QUIZ 2
What Type of Investor Are You?

1. I keep track of my spending: *(circle one of the following)*

   a. Monthly
   b. Annually
   c. When I run into a problem

2. Do I feel that I am doing well financially as long as my check doesn't bounce? *(answer yes or no)*

3. Do I plan and save for big purchases? *(answer yes or no)*

4. Do I buy on a whim and then return my purchases once I have the opportunity to reflect? *(answer yes or no)*

5. Do I buy investments with a low rate of return if they come with a guarantee? *(answer yes or no)*

6. Last time I ate at a restaurant: *(circle one of the following)*

   a. I read the entire menu, analyzing the content of each dish.
   b. I ordered steak because I like steak.
   c. I waited to see what my friends ordered before making my choice.

7. When tipping my server, it is most important to: *(circle one of the following)*

   a. Be accurate — tipping a predetermined percent.
   b. Be general — tipping by rounding up to the nearest approximate number.
   c. Tip based on my feelings about the service.

Cassie, Sam, and Matt completed Quiz 2 to identify their investment styles. Let's see how you compare.

If you are like Sam and answered yes to questions 1a, 3, 6a, and 7a, you are a Geek Investor.

The **Geek Investor** is a stickler for details and data. While it is good to be thorough with research, if taken to the extreme, you may forget to take your personal situation and goals into account when making investment decisions. As a Geek Investor, you can be hit with analysis paralysis, which means you have trouble making decisions because you cannot help thinking there is always more research to be done.

Rather than overwhelming yourself and spending too much time digging through content, as a Geek Investor, you should limit yourself to a few reliable sources. If you have a tendency to delay acting on your financial goals, make a list of pros and cons, give yourself a deadline, and stick to it.

While you may be great at budgeting, you might benefit from working with a financial planner who can help you distance yourself from your day-to-day transactions and help you recognize spending and saving trends over time. Having a comprehensive financial plan will satisfy the analytic investor's need for detail.

If you are like Cassie, and answered yes to questions 1b, 3, 5, 6b, and 7b, you are a Cautious Investor.

The **Cautious Investor** prefers to buy Guaranteed Investment Certificates (GIC) and Certificates of Deposit (CD) for long-term investing goals even if the rate of return is low. As a cautious investor, you may be missing out on growth opportunities for your long-term investments. While this approach can be less stressful, if you're able to consistently save enough to meet your financial goals, you will have to save more money than the Geek or Emotional Investor to achieve the same results.

The Cautious Investor will benefit from the principals of diversification and dollar cost averaging. Crucial to this type of investor is the advice of a financial planner who will assist in the selection of a prudent diversified fund with a track history of delivering results that exceed what can be earned with GICs and CDs.

To avoid falling into a set-it-and-forget-it routine and ending up with outdated and unsuccessful strategies for investing and saving, review your strategies at least once a year. For example, the investment plan you put in place five years ago might not be on pace to fund the goals you are working so hard to achieve. It is important to meet with your financial planner at least once a year.

If you are like Matt, and answered yes to questions 1c, 2, 4, 6c, and 7c, you are an Emotional Investor.

The **Emotional Investor** is reactionary, often making financial decisions based on what is happening at the moment and ignoring long-term needs and goals. You might look at it as "I am too young to think about putting aside a few dollars for retirement, it just seems so far away" or "I am healthy so why should I worry about a medical emergency?" As you saw with Matt, he discovered the hard way the importance of an emergency fund and an insurance plan.

Emotional Investors can benefit from a solid financial plan. Create two lists, one for short-term goals (e.g., vacation or vehicle purchase), and one for long-term goals (e.g., saving for retirement). Then set up savings accounts for each goal. To ensure each goal is properly funded consistently, it is best to set up automatic deposits to each account. Be sure to include a savings account for emergencies, and keep these funds away from debit card access.

To monitor his spending, Matt should use a debit card instead of cash and look at his account online at least once a month for the next six months until he understands where his money is going.

The Emotional Investor is the one most likely to buy high and sell low. Working with a financial planner can help prevent you from making impulsive changes to your investments and asset allocations that you may regret later. A planner will help to ease your worries about investments and keep you on track to meet your short- and long-term goals with appropriate investments for each.

CHAPTER TWELVE

Get Financial Help

* Read this if you are now working and ready to make important financial decisions regarding your insurance and/or investments.

* Read this if you want help choosing and hiring financial advisors that are right for you.

* Read this if you want to better understand the financial industry, how advisors are paid, and the resources available to you.

While growing up you had the benefit of teachers, tutors, and coaches, so why should adulthood be any different? Superior results are easier to achieve with good advice and the help of a coach. In this chapter you will learn to source the expert help you need and how to hire your own financial professionals.

1. Do-It-Yourself and Group Learning

Like your fitness program, your first introduction to financial planning may be a do-it-yourself approach. This is generally most helpful when you are looking to increase your general knowledge. There are many sources of advice for do-it-yourself financial planning such as banks, credit unions, investment firms, insurers, and mutual fund companies who offer useful tools and advice online.

The group approach would include programs offered through your community college or YMCA.

You may want to look at the website www.mint.com (in the US), and www.mint.com/canada (in Canada). Mint offers a free online money management tool that is easy to use. *The Wall Street Journal* called it one of the best online tools for personal finance.

2. Hiring an Advisor

When you want to optimize your results with your exercise regime, it can be tremendously valuable to hire a personal trainer; someone who will share strategies, and coach and encourage you to go on to the next level. The same is true of your financial life plan. A financial planner acts as your coach. He or she will prepare a multistep program designed to help you achieve your specific goals while establishing the good habits to reach those goals. Like a good coach, he or she will keep you focused, monitor your progress, and help you to stay on track.

A recent report titled "The Value of Advice" showed the value of using a financial advisor.[1] For households with annual earnings of $35,000 to $54,000, those who used a financial advisor on average had savings of $123,348. The households who did not have a financial advisor averaged only $27,104 in savings. That is a 78 percent difference! Not only did these savers have more to invest, they were more likely to take advantage of tax savings, putting more money back into their pockets.

The following are the benefits of working with a financial planner:

- Help you to establish realistic goals.
- Create a comprehensive financial plan outlining the actions and steps required to achieve your goals.
- Provide tax-savvy saving ideas.
- Protect you from the financial risk with solid insurance advice and products.
- Provide you with solid investment advice ensuring a well-diversified investment portfolio.

---

[1] Sources News Release, "IFIC Releases Report on the Value of Advice," www.sources.com/Releases/NR945.htm, (2010), accessed June 2011.

- Work with other professionals as needed, such as your accountant, banker, lawyer, or mortgage broker helping you to achieve optimal results.

- If you do not already work with other professionals, a financial advisor can help you to find suitable expertise.

- Gives you more time, which allows you to focus on your own area of expertise or to spend your leisure time doing something you enjoy.

Similar to a personal trainer, hiring a financial planner to coach you requires commitment on your part. The financial planner's professional advice will be of little value if you are not prepared follow through and implement the action steps he or she provides.

2.1 Selecting an advisor who can meet your needs

Good choices for early career developers like yourself may include talking to your parents' advisor, your local banker, and a financial advisor licensed to sell life insurance and mutual funds. We will explore these options fully later, but first ask yourself: "What kind of advice do I want and who is best qualified to help me? "

The world of financial planning can be confusing because there are so many designations, and so many ways to work and be paid. Many advisors call themselves "financial planners" when, more accurately, they should call themselves either "investment advisors" or "insurance advisors."

Generally, an *advisor* is one who gives advice on a specific or particular area of finances and is compensated, usually with commissions at the time the client makes a purchase of whatever product (e.g., insurance, mutual fund, stocks, bonds) the advisor sells.

A *planner* may give the same advice and be paid in the same way, but the difference is that a planner provides advice beyond the scope of the product being sold. Anyone who calls themselves a financial planner should provide a *plan*. The plan will include action items on how to achieve a set of goals as outlined by the client and should include advice for minimizing taxation, how much and what kind of insurance to buy, as well as how much money needs to be saved, at what rate of return, and for how long.

If you are looking for a planner, one of the very best credentials available is the Certified Financial Planner (CFP). The Certified

Financial Planners designation (CFP) is recognized internationally as the mark of a competent, ethical, and professional financial planner. CFPs are found in all areas of financial services. They may work for banks, credit unions, insurance companies, investment firms, accounting firms, full-service financial planning firms, stock brokerage firms, or their own private practice.

CFPs who work in the banking, insurance, or investment industry may prepare a full financial plan at no expense to you, since the commission from the sale of products you buy pays for this service. Some CFPs work on an hourly or fee-for-service basis. These professionals do not sell products but rather are paid for their time. Be sure to ask how your advisor is paid and how much it will cost you.

You will find a list of all CFPs in good standing at the following websites:

- United States: Certified Financial Planner Board of Standards, www.cfp.net
- Canada: Financial Planning Standards Council (FPSC), www.fpsc.ca/directory-cfp-professionals-good-standing

Quiz 3 is designed to help you better understand your needs. Once you have answered the questions you will be in a better position to select the right coach for you. When looking for a financial planner look for the CFP designation, which is your assurance that your financial planner is a highly trained individual who is knowledgeable and capable of creating a financial plan that will lead to the achievement of your goals.

Based on your answers in Quiz 3, the following is a list of the financial advisors most likely to be interested in your business and what you can expect from them.

Question 1: If you are a student or recent graduate who is not working, the advisor who can best help you at this stage of your life is a *career counselor*. If you are employed and want help achieving your three- to five-year goals, you would benefit from the services of a *financial planner*.

Question 2: If you are worried and losing sleep over how to pay your debts, you should book an appointment with the *credit manager* at your bank. Having an honest discussion about your ability to meet your debt obligations will put your banker or credit card company in a better position to help you restructure your loans. If this is not

QUIZ 3
What Type of Financial Advisor Suits Your Needs?

1. I am — *(add a checkmark to one or more of the following)*

   ☐ a student
   ☐ a recent graduate
   ☐ employed

2. Debt: I am worried about my ability to pay my student and/or consumer loans. *(answer yes or no)*

3. Insurance benefits *(add a checkmark to one or more of the following)*

   ☐ My employer offers a comprehensive health and disability insurance program, but I do not understand it.
   ☐ My employer does *not* offer a comprehensive health and disability insurance program.
   ☐ I have a family and worry about my ability to care for them in the event of an illness, disability, or death.

4. Goal planning *(add a checkmark to one of the following)*

   ☐ I have clear goals for the next five to ten years and have established a savings plan to meet those goals.
   ☐ I need help setting realistic goals and I am unsure of the best strategies to meet my five- to ten-year goals.

5. I need help creating and sticking to a budget. *(answer yes or no)*

6. Savings *(add a checkmark to one of the following)*

   ☐ I have some savings, but I am unsure of which investments to choose to meet my goals
   ☐ I am having difficulty sticking to a savings plan.

7. The amount of money I have currently saved to reach my ten-year goal: *(add a checkmark to one of the following)*

   ☐ Less than $5,000
   ☐ Between $5,000 and $50,000
   ☐ I am prepared to add money to my savings each and every month. The amount I can save each month is:

   o Less than $50
   o More than $50

8. I am interested in learning how to reduce my income taxes. *(answer yes or no)*

9. I plan to buy a home in the next five years and I will need to use my savings for the deposit. *(answer yes or no)*

possible, you may need the services of a *credit counselling agency* that will provide advice on how to manage your bills and debts.

Question 3: If you are employed full time, you could benefit from the services of a *life and health insurance agent* who will work with you to review the health and retirement benefits offered by your employer (see Chapter 9). If you are self-employed, or your employer does not offer benefits, a *licensed insurance agent* will help you find the right coverage to protect you and your family's health and future income.

Questions 4, 5, and 6: Working with a *financial planner*, in particular, will help you clarify your goals. A qualified financial planner will provide you with a clear list of action steps outlining the best strategies to achieve your goals. He or she will also help you complete a budget and show you how to meet your savings goals. If your goals, budget, or savings targets are unrealistic, a good planner will tell you so, and help you to devise a more realistic plan. As a new career builder, you will find qualified CFPs in the banking and insurance sector who are eager to work with you.

Question 7: If you have savings set aside for your mid- to long-term future goals, you could benefit from the help of an *investment advisor* who offers investment advice and products.

Assuming your parents are happy with their *financial advisor*, using your parents' advisor can make good sense. First, the advisor comes with a good character reference — your parents. Second, no matter how small your account is, you will receive VIP treatment. That is because the advisor sees you as the most important link to keeping your parents happy. As the heir to your parents' fortune, you are a VIP in waiting!

Investment advisors are generally paid a commission for selling you a product. For mutual funds, the cost of the purchase is embedded in the fees you pay to the mutual fund company. Part of these fees cover the cost that the mutual fund company incurs to manage the money, and the balance goes to your advisor and the firm where he or she works. When buying or selling stocks, a fee is charged for each transaction. Before choosing investments, ask for an explanation of the fees.

Question 8: For basic tax-saving ideas the services of a CFP can be useful. For more in-depth tax advice and preparation of your tax returns, you will need the services of a *tax planner* such as a Certified Public Accountant (CPA) in the United States or Chartered Accountant (CA) in Canada.

If your affairs are simple (e.g., you have a salaried or hourly job), you may choose to complete your tax return with the help of a software program, or you may engage the services of a tax preparation firm.

If your affairs are complex (e.g., you are self-employed or earn commissions or stock options), you would be wise to hire an accountant (i.e., CPA or CA) to assist you with tax planning and completion of your tax return. Using an accountant can save you many dollars in taxes each year.

You will pay either a set fee negotiated in advance for the service delivered, or an hourly rate billed after the service is completed. To avoid an unpleasant surprise, be sure to ask for an estimate in advance. Compensation should *not* be based on the size of your tax refund!

Question 9: If you plan to buy a home in the next five years and need to use your savings for the deposit, the safest place to keep your house money is in a savings account. Even if the interest paid on this account is low, your primary concern should be the security of your savings. Ask your banker to confirm the highest insured amount for your savings. Generally, this amount is up to $100,000.

Once you are closer to your home purchase goal, you will need the help of a reputable real estate agent to identify the home of your dreams. Frequently your real estate agent will introduce you to a lawyer who specializes in real estate law. You will also need the services of a mortgage broker or your bank to arrange for financing.

A mortgage broker is the person you rely on when you need to borrow funds to buy a condo, a house, or another piece of real estate. The mortgage broker's job is to shop the market for you and bring you the best rate. Your banker also provides mortgages with the funds coming from the bank. You would be wise to shop around for the best rate. A good mortgage broker can save you thousands of dollars in interest payments.

It is a good idea to interview a few mortgage brokers before selecting one, or get a referral from someone you know who has used one and was satisfied with this person's services in the past.

Generally your mortgage broker is paid a commission by the lender. You do not pay for this service out of your pocket. Rather, the cost is part of the rate you pay for the loan.

2.2 Choosing your financial advisor

I highly recommend you become familiar with the professionals who can help you to achieve your goals. Hire the advisors you feel comfortable with and upon whose advice you can rely. A good advisor is always willing to admit where his or her area of expertise ends and is willing to seek the advice of the other professionals as required.

When looking for a financial planner or advisor, you want someone you can relate to, and someone who understands you and your goals. Speaking to your friends and family may help you to identify a financial planner with whom they enjoy working.

You also want to hire the person with the best qualifications and reputation. You can check out the professional standings of advisors you are interested in by going to their association websites. Each financial advisor is part of a licensing regulatory body. Ask which professional association your potential advisor is affiliated with and do an online search.

Take the time to interview at least three financial planners or advisors. This will allow you to compare each advisor and find the one who best understands your goals and is willing to count you among their valued clients. Book the interview appointment in their offices; this will give you the opportunity to see how professional the office environment is.

Once you have chosen your financial planner, you will need to be ready to work with him or her by providing timely information. Arrive at the meeting prepared for the day's agenda. Be prepared to ask lots of questions. Financial planning can be very complex and your advisor is there to simplify the process, provide clarity, and give you peace of mind. If you are unsure of a recommendation or a product, keep asking questions until you understand how implementing his or her recommendations will bring you closer to your goals.

When dealing with your advisors, you will find there is a lot of paperwork. Try not to feel rushed. Take your time, and ask your professional to take the time to go through the paperwork with you explaining what you do not understand. If he or she is not prepared to do so, take the documents home where you can read them in peace, make notes, and return with a list of questions. Never sign a document you have not read or understood!

Your relationship with your financial planner or advisor will last many years when the lines of communication are kept open. Your advisor is your coach showing the way towards achieving your goals. You can count on him or her to keep you focused financially and on track!

Exercise 11 is a list of questions to assist you when you are interviewing prospective financial planners.

EXERCISE 11
Questions to Ask a Potential Financial Advisor

Background

1. What is your educational background?

2. What financial planning designations do you hold?

3. Do you have the CFP designation?

4. How long have you been a financial planner?

5. Has a complaint ever been lodged against you?

Financial Planning Services and Products

6. Do you provide a written analysis of my financial situation?

7. Do you provide recommendations showing me how to best reach my goals?

8. Do you provide advice and/or products in the following areas:
   - ☐ Goal setting
   - ☐ Budgeting
   - ☐ Debt management
   - ☐ Insurance analysis and recommendations
   - ☐ Investment recommendations
   - ☐ Tax-saving ideas

Service Levels

9. How long can I expect to wait before my call is returned?

10. Will I be working with you, or with one of your associates? If I will be working with one of your associates, who is this person and may I meet him or her?

11. Are you prepared to meet annually to review my plan?

12. How often can I expect to hear from you during the year?

Compensation

13. How are you paid? Do you charge an hourly fee? Or are you paid by commission?

14. Does your firm offer you a financial incentive for recommending certain products?

15. What fees (if any) will I have to pay if I choose to sell an investment or move my account?

3. Review Your Financial Plan Annually

Just like your vehicle, your financial plan will require a regular checkup. Your financial planner will most likely suggest an annual review. He or she will likely want to review the following questions with you:

- Have there been any changes in your career or lifestyle which may impact your finances?

- Have your goals changed? If so, how?

- Will you be making a major purchase in the next year which would impact your cash flow?

- How are you doing with your budget and are you able to stay on track?

- Have you been able to keep your savings toward your goals on track?

- Have you been satisfied with his or her planning services?

Your financial planner will more than likely share ideas that can save you money on taxes. He or she will also review your health, disability, and life insurance needs at your annual meeting as well as review your investments and make recommendations for rebalancing your portfolio as required.

At your annual meeting you should ask the following questions:

1. Based on my goals as described to you, how am I doing?

2. What more do I need to do to achieve my goals? What could I do better?

3. Why are you recommending this particular insurance or investment to me?

4. How does your recommendation (insurance or investment) meet my goals?

5. Are there other choices that would help me reach my goals?

6. What will it cost me now, and in the future?

7. What, if any, are the costs to me if I implement your recommendation?

8. Can I get my money back? What if I need it sooner or change my mind?

9. How has this investment performed in the past? Is it realistic to expect the same performance in the future?

10. What are the risks involved with following, or not following, your recommendations?

Over time you and your financial planner will come to know each other very well. The better you know each other, the better your planner will understand your goals and the coaching you need to achieve those goals. Many financial planners measure the success of their client relationships by their longevity. Your planner is in it for the long term and will do his or her best to see you succeed.

CHAPTER THIRTEEN

Buying a Vehicle

* Read this if you are planning to purchase a vehicle in the near future.

* Read this if you are not sure whether to buy a new vehicle or a used one.

* Read this if you wonder whether you should buy or lease your next vehicle.

Vehicles are a lousy investment. There, I said it.

If you recall in Chapter 8, you listed your vehicle as an asset, but of all your assets your vehicle is the worst performing asset. It is the only asset that is guaranteed to reduce in value over time. Your savings account can be relied on to grow by the interest earned. You add money to your investment accounts in anticipation of future growth in the investment markets. If you own a home, it too will grow in value. However, a vehicle will never be worth more than it was the day you bought it and drove away with it!

If there is one message to take away from reading this chapter it is that vehicles are lousy investments. Day after day your vehicle depreciates in value. You will spend many thousands of dollars on vehicles over your lifetime, and every time you make a vehicle purchase, your net worth will have dropped the following day.

If you purchase a brand new car, as you drive off the car lot and wave to your friendly salesperson, your brand new vehicle just lost as much as 10 percent of its value. In three years it will likely be worth less than half of what you paid for it!

If vehicles are a poor investment, they are also a big cost. Whether you rent or own your home, the cost of owning and operating a vehicle is likely your second largest monthly expense. The average car today is selling for $20,000 to $35,000. If you are like many people, you will make a vehicle purchase every 5 years for the next 45 years. Assuming an average cost of $35,000, you will purchase more than $315,000 of vehicles. For a two-vehicle family, the number doubles. This does not include insurance, gas, regular maintenance, or repairs. You may not invest as much in your family home. Clearly this is a big expense and one to take seriously.

1. Do Your Research before Buying a Vehicle

In my experience, there are few events less pleasurable than the process of selecting, negotiating, and choosing a payment method for a vehicle. Be prepared to spend a reasonable amount of time to ensure you are well-informed, enabling you to make a wise choice.

When it comes to buying a vehicle, the three most important things to consider are "research, research, and research." If you are still unsure, more research is in order. You will need to research the following:

- what make, model, and year is the best value for your hard-earned money;

- whether you will buy a new vehicle or a used one; and

- whether you should purchase or lease.

Luckily, help is available and you can rely on the expertise of several sources, many of them online. When it comes to selecting the best make and model, try these websites:

- Consumer Reports offers ratings for thousands of products from appliances to recreation items. They provide vehicle-buying advice for both new and used cars and trucks. You will need to register and become a member: www.consumerreports.org.

- Phil Edmonston is an amazing consumer advocate and author of the Lemon-Aid guidebooks. He is dedicated to helping consumers make better choices when purchasing both new and used vehicles. He offers the following websites: www.edmunds.com/car-reviews and www.lemonaidcars.com.

Both of these resources will provide you with more information than you care to know about selecting and maintaining a vehicle. Why do the legwork yourself when the research has already been done for you? Selecting one of the top three rated vehicles in your price range will help you to narrow the range of possibilities and make a choice you will be happy with.

2. Should You Buy a New or Used Vehicle?

The draw of a new car can be overpowering, but before you pay your deposit to the salesperson, consider that vehicles depreciate the most in the first year. It is possible to acquire a recent model car with low mileage and a good warranty, while putting some significant savings in your pocket.

When researching new vehicles versus used, ask yourself the following questions.

- Knowing that this vehicle will depreciate by at least 10 percent as soon as I drive off the lot, how important is it to me to drive a new vehicle?

- Am I willing to pay significantly more to drive a brand new vehicle?

- How much will this vehicle be worth in one, three, and five years from now? (Some cars keep their value, while others lose value quickly.)

- How much can I save by buying last year's model? Or one that is now two or three years old?

- How long do I plan to own this vehicle?

- How long does the typical purchaser keep this type of vehicle?

- What is the manufacturer's warranty?

- If I am buying a used car, how much longer will it run?

3. Should You Buy or Lease?

When making arrangements to pay for your vehicle, there are three choices available to you:

- Pay cash

- Make a deposit and borrow the balance

- Lease

Unless you are purchasing an older model, very few young adults can afford to pay cash. The remaining choices are to borrow to make a purchase, or lease. Which is right for you? Each of these options is quite different so let's review the options first.

3.1 Buying

When you purchase a vehicle, you are making the decision to become the owner of the vehicle. You and the seller have agreed on a price. When you buy a vehicle, it belongs to you. As the owner of the car, you are responsible for its upkeep or lack thereof. You have the right to sell it or transfer the ownership to another person (assuming your lender has approved of this in advance).

If you are borrowing, your lender will provide you with the funds to make the purchase. First your lender will need you to complete the following steps and it will likely require security for the money:

- You will be asked to make a deposit. This deposit reduces your lender's risk. Remember, your vehicle is a depreciating asset, and your lender would prefer not to repossess your vehicle while your loan exceeds the value of it.

- Complete a loan application proving your ability to make the required payments. Your lender will need to see proof of income and a net worth statement. The lender will also need to know what you pay for monthly expenses. Aren't you glad you read the chapters on cash flow (Chapter 7) and net worth (Chapter 8)?

- Your lender will check your credit rating to ensure that it is not taking on a poor risk. The higher your credit score, the easier it will be for you to find a lender, and the lower rate of interest you will be asked to pay. It is a good idea to shop around for the best rate.

Before you make any decisions about buying a vehicle, there are five things you must know:

What is the *final* price for the vehicle? This will have to be negotiated between you and the vendor.

- How much of a deposit is required?

- What rate of interest will be charged on the borrowed amount?

- Term of your loan (how many monthly payments will you be required to pay)?

- How much will your monthly payments be?

If math is not your strong point, take a basic calculator with you and go home, to the parking lot, or to the restroom and do the math for yourself. If it does not make sense to you, go back and ask for a full explanation. If you have to do this more than twice, the third time I would conclude you are working with the wrong salesperson. Leave and never return again. You deserve to work with a representative who respects you enough to be honest with you and who is prepared to answer every single one of your questions, no matter how tedious.

3.2 Leasing

The major difference between buying and leasing is that with a lease, you are *not* the owner of the vehicle. Leasing a vehicle is similar to renting an apartment. Your landlord owns the apartment and you have the use of the apartment for the duration of your lease. Your total payments will be less than the value of the vehicle since your payments are only enough to pay for the expected depreciation over the term of the lease plus the cost of financing.

Similar to your apartment, you are responsible for the care and cleaning of your vehicle. If you damage the vehicle, you will be required to repair it to its "like new" condition.

At the end of the lease you will return the car in good condition to your dealer. At that time you may choose to purchase the vehicle at its remaining "residual" value as set out in your contract, or pass the dealer the keys and the car. Other than making your monthly payment, returning the vehicle in good condition with no more than the agreed-upon mileage, your obligations are complete. Lease payments are lower than loan payments because you are making payments on the amount the vehicle is expected to depreciate over the term of the lease, compared to buying where you pay for the entire vehicle over the term of the loan.

Before you make any decisions about leasing a vehicle, there are eight things you must know:

- What is the final price of the vehicle? Yes, this is still important because your monthly lease amount is based on this figure. Even if you are leasing, you have the right to negotiate your best price.

- How much of a deposit is required?

- What rate of interest will be charged on the lease amount?

- Term of your lease (how many monthly payments will you be required to make)?

- How much will your monthly payments be?

- How many miles/kilometers are you allowed before being required to pay a penalty? What is the charge per mile/kilometer if you exceed the maximum?

- What is the residual value? This is the amount the vehicle will be worth at the end of the lease term.

- Total your deposit and the monthly lease payments. Does this total bring you close to the cost of buying the car outright? If yes, this is a poor lease offer.

You need the same information as if you were going to purchase the vehicle plus a few more items. Still, the mathematics of leasing should not be beyond comprehension. Do *not* sign a lease without knowing the answers to the questions above.

If you would like more help understanding your lease options go to http://LeaseGuide.com. This website offers an excellent explanation of leasing and what to look out for. You can even purchase (for a modest amount) a lease kit which is designed to assist you in working through the math of leasing.

Want to save money on a lease? It is now possible to assume someone else's lease. Every year people enter into lease agreements that they cannot honor. When you assume someone else's lease, you are taking on the responsibility for the remaining payments. This saves you the cost of the initial deposit. If you are interested, try the following websites:

- http://swapalease.com

- www.LeaseBusters.com

Quiz 4 will help you decide whether buying or leasing is right for you.

QUIZ 4
Should You Buy or Lease a Vehicle?

Question	Yes	No
1. Do you want the lowest possible monthly payment?		
2. Do you want the newest vehicle available?		
3. Are you proud of your possessions, your personal appearance, and your public image?		
4. Do you drive a similar amount of miles each year?		
5. Do you know anything about the mechanics of a vehicle?		
6. Do you worry about an expensive repair, or would you have trouble coming up with the cash to pay for such a repair?		
7. Do you plan to keep your vehicle for no longer than 36 to 48 months?		
8. Do you hate the idea of selling your vehicle on your own?		
9. Do you have a stable and secure source of income?		
10. Are you confident in your ability to make the deposit and the monthly payments?		
11. Do you drive more than the average driver?		
12. Do you plan to pay off your vehicle loan as fast as possible, even if it means higher monthly payments?		
13. Do you plan to keep your vehicle for the long term (i.e., five to ten years)?		
14. Are last week's dirty dishes still sitting in the sink and is the pile of soiled clothing in the doorway blocking your view of the laundry room?		
15. Do you have a limited budget, which means you only have the funds to buy an older vehicle (i.e., five years old or older), and do you have some mechanical ability?		
16. Is your idea of a great date sitting on the side of the highway while your partner passes you wrenches as you repair your vehicle?		

If you answered "yes" to questions 1 through 10, consider leasing your next vehicle. Leasing works for you because you take good care of your possessions, allowing you to honor the terms of the lease agreement and return the vehicle in good condition. Leasing generally means you will be driving a recent model vehicle with full warranties, giving you the peace of mind that you will not need to pay for expensive mechanical repairs. Leasing allows you to drive a newer model vehicle at the lowest possible monthly cost.

Lease payments should be approximately one-third lower than purchasing loan payments. The reason leasing has a lower monthly cost is because you are not financing the entire cost of the vehicle but rather, paying for the expected depreciation while you drive it. When you return the vehicle, there is a residual value you did not pay for. Of course, since you do not own the vehicle, you cannot modify it or sell it.

If you answered "yes" to questions 8 through 16, consider buying your next vehicle. Buying works for you because you plan to keep your vehicle for the long term (i.e., eight years or more).

If you answered "yes" to question 11 and you drive more than the average driver, you would be penalized by the mileage restrictions when leasing a car. Those who drive much less than normal can expect their vehicle to keep its value and last longer than average.

If your housekeeping skills leave something to be desired, your vehicle is likely to get similar treatment. As the owner of your vehicle, no one will question how you care for or maintain it. You have some mechanical ability and may wish to do your own maintenance and repairs.

If you answered "no" to questions 9 and 10, you should not enter into either a purchase or lease contract at this time. Both buying and leasing requires that you have the ability to meet your payment commitments. Since both buying and leasing terms run from 24 to 60 months it is important you have the financial stability to meet this financial obligation. If not, it is you who will be the sucker disposing of your vehicle under duress while someone else negotiates themselves a sweet deal on your vehicle.

Surprising Tip: Can you guess what the typical American millionaire drives? The answer may surprise you. According to Thomas J. Stanley, co-author of *The Millionaire Next Door*, "Most millionaires are not driving this year's model. Only a minority drive a foreign motor vehicle. An even smaller minority drive foreign luxury cars."

Choose your vehicles carefully. Do not overspend for the privilege of driving an asset whose value drops faster than nightfall on a winter's day.

CHAPTER FOURTEEN

Buying a Home

* Read this if you are planning to buy a home in the next few years.

At some point in your life you will consider making your first home purchase. This may be done alone or with your spouse. In either case, the purchase of a home could be the largest single investment of your life! In addition, unless you win the lottery, it is most likely that it will take 25 years or more to pay off your mortgage.

The advantages of buying a home include the following:

- Instead of paying rent for the rest of your life, you will eventually pay off your home. After your home is paid off, those monthly payments can go to something else (e.g., savings account for retirement, vacation).

- By eventually owning your home, your net worth will increase.

- You will have a place that you can call your own.

- Owning your own home will inspire you and lead to a sense of accomplishment and pride.

The disadvantages of buying a home include the following:

- Real estate markets often go through hot and cold periods. In a hot market, prices are rising, and it is easier to sell a home in a shorter time frame. Cold markets are just the opposite — prices fall, and it is sometimes difficult to sell a home within a reasonable time frame. It is not unusual for people to sell their home at a loss in a cold market if they are forced to sell. For this reason, you should only consider purchasing your first home if your job is secure and you can weather the storm in both hot and cold real estate markets.

- If you are buying your first home with your boyfriend or girl-friend, you should be confident that your relationship with each other is on a solid footing. Who wants to purchase a home and then be forced to sell it two years later if the relationship breaks down?

- Buying your first home will be an emotional journey. You will likely experience some frustration looking at many homes and coming to grips with costs, your likes and dislikes, etc. Needless to say, emotions can run high if you and your spouse or partner are both involved. That said, the effort you put in will be well worth it if you view this as a long-term commitment to your future.

1. Terms You'll Need to Know

Before we begin the home-buying discussion, let's go over a few terms you need to become familiar with when buying a home:

- **Down payment:** The down payment is the difference between the purchase price of the home and the amount of the price that is being financed. For example, the purchase price is $200,000 and your lender agrees to finance $180,000. Thus, your down payment is $20,000 ($200,000 less $180,000).

- **Mortgage:** A mortgage is a loan against your new home. Note that you pledge the home as security to provide for repayment of your loan.

- **Mortgage amortization:** This is the number of years over which the lender spreads the loan. This is normally between 25 and 35 years.

- **Mortgage broker:** In addition to talking to your bank about a loan, you may save money by using a mortgage broker. Unlike a bank, mortgage brokers work on behalf of several lenders and try to provide you with the best interest rate available.

- **Mortgage term:** A mortgage term is applicable in Canada. The meaning of the word "term" depends on whether you obtain a mortgage in Canada versus the United States.

  In Canada, even though the mortgage may be amortized over a long period (e.g., 25 years) the *term* is usually shorter (e.g., six months to five years or more). When the term expires, the balance owing on the mortgage can be repaid or the lender generally renews the mortgage at the current interest rates. The interest rates (and, thus, your monthly payments) can go up if interest rates increase.

  In the United States, home buyers may opt for a *fixed rate mortgage*. These are often referred to as "plain vanilla" mortgage products because of their ease of comprehension among borrowers. In this case, the reference to *term* is different than in Canada. Specifically, both the term and amortization period are the same, meaning the loan may be spread out and repaid over 30 years and the interest rate also stays the same for 30 years.

- **Mortgage high-ratio insurance:** This is a cost to you but it protects the *lender*. If you don't have 20 percent of the lesser of the purchase price or appraised value of the property, your mortgage must be insured against payment default by a mortgage insurer. Most first-time purchasers have no choice but to accept this cost to purchase a home.

- **Closing costs:** There are various expenses associated with purchasing your first home which most buyers overlook. Examples include appraisal fees, legal or notary fees and disbursements, land transfer taxes, as well as adjustments for prepaid property taxes or condominium common expenses.

- **Move-in costs:** This is another overlooked item by first-time purchasers. It can include such items as moving costs, painting and upgrades, purchasing appliances, changing door locks, etc.

- **Appraisal:** When you apply for a loan for your new home, the lender may require that an independent appraiser determine the fair value of the property. This is a cost that you must pay. The appraiser's value of the home can be higher or lower than the price you have agreed to purchase the home.

2. Types of Housing

This is your first home purchase and the primary factors which will influence how much you can spend are as follows:

- How much cash you have saved as a deposit or down payment toward the total purchase price.

- How much of a mortgage you can afford in order to purchase your first home.

Essentially, you are starting at the bottom, just like when you bought your first car. You cannot expect to buy a new Mercedes-Benz convertible that costs $100,000 plus as your first car! Your dream home comes later in life as your income and savings increase. This is normal and to be expected.

Ask your parents to describe the first home they had. Ask them the same question about your grandparents. You may be surprised how modestly they lived when they purchased their first home.

There are many housing types; the three most common are briefly described in the following sections.

2.1 Single-family home

By far the most common form of housing in North America is the single-family detached home. The most important distinguishing factor which determines a single-family dwelling is that it sits on its own piece of land or lot and it is not attached to anyone else's residence. Because of this, it is generally the most expensive.

If you like to have your own space, and you are willing to accept the responsibilities such as cutting the lawn, trimming the bushes, shoveling snow, and general maintenance, then this is the ideal type of home for you. In this type of home, you can make changes such as the exterior or interior color and appearance.

2.2 Townhouse

Generally a townhouse is less expensive than a single-family home. A townhouse is a home that is attached to one or more other houses, but which sits directly on a parcel of land that you also own (if you don't own the land, it is a condominium).

If you like the idea of your own space, but you like the idea of not having to deal with most exterior maintenance, a townhouse may be the ideal dwelling for you. Townhouses usually have a small backyard or deck, which may be just about all the yard (and yard work) you need! If the idea of having neighbors close doesn't really bother you, go for it!

2.3 Condominium

A condominium is generally the least expensive. A condominium may be described as an apartment that you own. This makes you co-owner, with all of the other owners in the complex, of any common areas (e.g., roof, parking lot, play areas).

As an owner you must pay a monthly condo fee, which covers general repairs and maintenance to the common areas as well as building a cash reserve for future needs. In general, all exterior maintenance and repairs are the responsibility of the condominium although you will be charged for them. In cities with expensive real estate, a condominium may be the only option that you can afford!

If you prefer having nothing to do with exterior maintenance and repairs, and you like the safety of nearby neighbors, then living in a condo may be the right choice for you.

3. Borrowing to Buy Your New Home

Most homeowners borrow money for their mortgage based on an amortization period of 30 years. It is amazing how much money you can save by reducing this to 25 years. Let's take a look:

- Assumed mortgage amount: $200,000

- Assumed interest rate: 5 percent

- Mortgage payments over 30 years: $1,074.64 per month

- Mortgage payments over 25 years: $1,169.18 per month

By eliminating your mortgage five years earlier your monthly mortgage payment will increase by $94.54. How much will you save in interest by eliminating your mortgage five years earlier? $35,756![1] See Sample 16.

SAMPLE 16
Mortgage Comparison

Mortgage Payment Duration	Monthly	Annual	Total
Over 30 years	$1,073.64	$12,884	$386,510
Over 25 years	1,169.18	14,030	350,754
		Savings in Interest	$35,756

When buying your first home, you will likely have a choice to make regarding the type of mortgage that is available. While there are numerous options available in both the United States and Canada, the two most common are briefly described below:

- **Fixed-rate mortgage:** The interest rate is locked in by the lender. Thus, your payments remain the same for the mortgage term and you know where you stand. Why would anyone choose a fixed-rate mortgage if the interest rate is higher? In short, some people like stability versus uncertainty.

- **Variable-rate or an adjustable-rate mortgage:** The interest rate can and does change. Thus, your payments will vary over time. Why would anyone choose a variable or adjustable rate mortgage? The interest rate is generally lower than a fixed-rate mortgage.

You have to decide if you want the stability of a fixed-rate mortgage, or if you're comfortable with the potential risks and rewards of a variable-rate mortgage. As of the date of writing this book, interest rates are at historic lows and there is reason to believe that the cost of borrowing will increase over time. Therefore, you could face higher mortgage payments if you choose a variable-rate or an adjustable-rate mortgage. Over the past few years, many homeowners in the United States have encountered mortgage problems due, in

---

[1] Mortgage Calculator, "Mortgage Calculator," www.mortgagecalculator.org, (2011), accessed June 2011.

part, to increasing mortgage payments associated with adjustable-rate mortgages. My recommendation is, if you can afford a fixed-rate mortgage, take it. You will not have to worry about potential increases in your monthly payment. Stability is more important than uncertainty.

Since this is your first home purchase, it is recommended that you make an appointment with your banker or mortgage broker to review your situation. You will be advised how much of a mortgage you can afford. This will determine how much you can pay for your first home.

In order to have some idea on how much of a mortgage you can afford, you can ask your lender to prequalify you. Qualification (or "prequalification" as it is often called) is an opinion that your income, assets, and current debts qualify you for a loan of some specified amount. That said, since this does not take your credit into account, the lender's opinion is not a commitment — just an opinion.

Once you have decided you will be looking at homes with plans to purchase, you can ask your lender for a preapproval letter for your mortgage. This involves verification of your personal information wherein the lender will ask for documentation to confirm your employment, the source of your down payment, and other aspects of your financial circumstances. This is more time-consuming than being prequalified and it carries more weight. Realtors will also consider this an advantage in dealing with you since you essentially passed the test to obtain your mortgage.

Whether you live in the United States or Canada, lenders use two different debt ratios to determine if you can afford your mortgage. These two debt ratios are:

- **Gross Debt Service (GDS) Ratio:** The percentage of gross income required to cover monthly payments associated with housing costs. Most lenders recommend that the GDS ratio be no more than 28 percent (in the US)[2] or 32 percent (in Canada)[3] of your gross (before tax) monthly income.

- **Total Debt Service (TDS) Ratio:** The percentage of gross income needed to cover monthly payments for housing and all other debts and financing obligations. The total should generally not exceed 36 percent (in the US)[2] or 37 percent (in Canada)[3] of gross monthly income.

[2] Interest.com, "Mortgage Rates," www.interest.com, (2011), accessed June 2011.

[3] TD Canada Trust, "Mortgages," www.tdcanadatrust.com/mortgages/glossary.jsp, (2011), accessed June 2011.

It is important to try to keep your GDS below 30 percent and your TDS below 36 percent.

Since this is a major financial commitment, it is important to have a safety net. If possible, you should have several months of income in a separate savings account that can be used in the event of an emergency or a period of difficulty.

Check the Resources on the CD included with this book for links to sources for mortgages and mortgage information.

4. The Importance of Location

The location of your home is likely the most important aspect which will affect future resale value. For example, which of the following would you prefer?

- Having your home situated next to a dangerous industry where toxic waste is common?

- Having your home situated in a planned residential community with parks, schools, and entertainment located nearby?

A good realtor will emphasize location. If you purchase a home that will appeal to the largest number of potential future home buyers, you will minimize potential negative influences on future resale value and maximize positive influences.

With your first home purchase, you will be faced with several different location choices. The first choice you will have to make is the community. Try to select a community that most people would want to live in since this "desirability" will add to future resale value.

The next choice is deciding on what area of the community you would like to live. Don't make the mistake of identifying a home simply because it is the least expensive alternative and offers more home for the money. Rather, it is generally smarter to purchase a smaller home in a superior area than to purchase a larger home located in an inferior location or distant from city services. This can be the most difficult choice for first-time buyers. You may regret being in an inferior area but you will not likely regret living in a more desirable place — even if the home is smaller.

5. Get What You Want without Overpaying

The following are a series of questions that you should ask your realtor when viewing a home you are interested in purchasing:

- **How long has the home been for sale?** This is important because in a normal market, homes are sold within 90 days of being listed. If a home you are looking at has been listed for sale for six months to one year or more, it may be overpriced and you should be careful not to offer too much.

- **When does the seller want to close the deal?** If the existing owner has bought another home, he or she may want a quick closing date to eliminate the cost of owning two homes. This could be an advantage to you if you offer a lower price but a closing date that is attractive to the seller.

- **Why are they selling?** This question will help you determine if the seller is motivated (i.e., the person *needs* to sell). For example, if the seller is under financial pressure and wants a quick sale, this will generally lead to a reduced price.

- **Has the seller received other offers?** A seller who has rejected several offers which are close to the asking price is likely hard to deal with.

- **Have there been any changes in the asking price?** If there have been reductions and there are still no buyers, this could be an opportunity to purchase the home at a discount.

The following are additional things to consider when negotiating:

- **Since this is your first home, it is not necessary for you to include a condition in an offer that you have to sell another home first.** This is a distinct advantage since it is a "clean offer." Use this to offer a lower price.

- **Ask the realtor to provide you with a competitive market analysis.** This depicts how much homes have sold for in the area. Drive by the sold homes yourself. This will assist you in understanding the values for similar homes so that you don't overpay.

- **If you make an offer to purchase a home, you should** *always* **make the offer conditional on obtaining a building inspection which is subject to your approval.** Although you will have to pay for the inspection, it protects you since you want to know the good, the bad, and the ugly of the home. The good will be okay, the bad can be dealt with, but the ugly may deter you from buying!

- **If your offer to purchase is accepted, you should go through the home with the inspector you hired and ask questions.** If he or she identifies items which require attention or work, ask for an estimate of the cost. You can then use this to your advantage by asking for a price adjustment if the cost is significant — basically a reduction from the price you offered before you go further.

- **If you and your spouse are considering making an offer on a home, my suggestion is that you discuss it together.** Once you have made a decision, advise your realtor on the amount, closing date, etc.

- **Don't be afraid to offer a lower price.** You can always increase your offer if you have to. That said, it could be dangerous to offend the seller by offering 40 percent less than the asking price.

EXERCISE 12
Steps for Purchasing Your First Home

The following steps will help you work through the home-buying process. Make a copy of this form to make notes on as you work through each step.

Step 1: Determine your sources of cash

Calculate how much cash you have:

Bank accounts	$ _____
Other sources	$ _____
Total Cash	**$ _____**

Step 2: Meet with a lender or mortgage broker

When you meet with a lender or mortgage broker, bring the following along with you:

- Details of your employment and income (i.e., last year's tax return and three recent pay stubs)
- Details of your savings and expenses (i.e., copies of your bank statements, investments, and letter from relatives if they plan to assist you with your down payment)
- Request estimates on closing costs (see Step 3)
- Request a mortgage preapproval letter

Step 3: Estimate the costs to close the home purchase

Lender processing fees (ask the lender)	$ _____
Lender other fees (ask the lender)	$ _____
Appraisal fee (ask the lender)	$ _____
Home inspection (ask the lender)	$ _____
Land transfer tax (ask the lender)	$ _____
Title insurance (ask the lender)	$ _____
Legal fees (ask the lender)	$ _____
Security deposit for utilities (contact the utility companies)	$ _____
Phone connection (contact the phone company)	$ _____
Mail redirect costs (contact the post office)	$ _____
Tax and heat adjustments on closing (budget $500 for now)	$ _____
Miscellaneous (budget $500 for now)	$ _____
Preliminary Estimate of Closing Costs	**$ _____**

Next, estimate the "other" costs when an offer is made and accepted:

Moving costs	$ _____
House insurance premium	$ _____
Painting and cleaning	$ _____
Appliance(s)	$ _____
Other: Contingency fund	$ _____
Other	$ _____
Total Other Costs	**$ _____**

Step 4: Calculate your housing affordability

How much can you afford to pay?

Your total cash sources (Step 1)		$ _____
Minus preliminary estimate of closing and other costs (Step 3)	−	$ _____
		$ _____
a. Cash left for down payment on your home		$ _____
b. Add the amount of mortgage that you can afford (Step 2)	+	$ _____
Approximate price you can pay for your first home (a + b)		**$ _____**

Step 5: Find a reputable realtor

- Obtain two to three referrals from family and friends
- Interview each realtor and select one you are comfortable with

Step 6: Choose a location

Have your realtor drive you through two or three neighborhoods that offer housing in your price range. When looking for a location, consider the following:

- Distance to work: Can you get by with one vehicle or do you need two?
- Ease of traffic
- Schools if you have children, or want to have children someday
- Proximity to parks
- Amenities (e.g., groceries, restaurants, entertainment)
- Lot sizes, privacy, presence of trees
- Is pride of ownership evident?
- Demographics: Approximate age of the residents, occupations, etc., in the neighborhood
- Important: What about the future resale value? Try to pick an area where everyone would like to be, even if it means a smaller home

Step 7: Inspecting homes listed for sale

How many homes should you see? Probably 50 to 75, mostly through open houses and appointments (with your realtor). Why so many? This is your first purchase. Seeing many homes for sale will be a huge benefit to you when it comes to —

- gauging what is good, average, and below average;
- getting what is important to you; and
- providing you with a "feel" for the market, pricing, and how much homes are selling for.

Note: Your realtor may not like the fact that you want to see 50 to 75 homes. You can inspect as many open houses as you want without requesting that your realtor be with you.

What should you look for? Try to find a home where the most expensive items have already been dealt with. Expensive items could include the following:

- Newer kitchen cabinets and plumbing
- New bathroom fixtures
- Newer electrical wiring
- Newer heating and air conditioning
- Newer roof and shingles
- Newer windows

If the painting and wallpaper is outdated, ignore this since it is usually easy to change. In fact, it is best if the colors are ugly since the home won't show as well and you can negotiate a lower price. However, if the floor plan is odd or downright awful, eliminate this listing since it is usually costly to change a floor plan.

If you see a home you like, ask your realtor what the following costs are for the home:

Operating costs	$ _____
Cost of property taxes	$ _____
Cost of heating and air conditioning	$ _____
Cost of electricity and utilities	$ _____

EXERCISE 12 – CONTINUED

You should also ask for the following:

- A list of upgrades and improvements to the home in the past three years.
- Are appliances included (e.g., fridge, stove, dishwasher, washer, and dryer)?
- Are the window coverings included? (They usually are, but it never hurts to ask.)
- What are the neighbors like (e.g., approximate age, children)?
- If there is a vacant lot near or across the street, you must find what it is zoned for and what it can be used for. You would regret your purchase if a new manufacturing plant was constructed across the street from your first home in the future and caused traffic problems and noise!

If the property is a condominium, you will need to find out the following:

- How much are the monthly common expenses? $ _____
- Have there been any "special assessments" in the last three years?
- If so, how much and for what purpose? $ _____
- Who is the property manager for the condominium corporation?
- Ask the realtor for a copy of the financial statements for the condominium corporation.
- Ask your realtor if the condominium's reserve requirements meet state or provincial requirements.
- Ask the realtor for copies of minutes of the annual meeting for the past three years. Are there any controversial items which have been noted that are of concern?
- What are the "rules and regulations" for the condominium? For example, does it permit pets? Are there restrictions on where you can park?

Step 8: Making an offer to purchase your first home

You will eventually see a potential home which appeals to you and your budget. Here are a few tips on how to proceed:

- Imagine that you are playing poker; in other words, do not reveal your cards to the other players.
- You will be emotional but try not to show it when viewing the home.
- Likewise, it is not prudent to display your emotions to your realtor. Always remember that your realtor's job is to sell you a home.
- After seeing this potential home for the first time, think about how you would like living there. Walk the neighborhood (yourself) in daytime and in the evening.
- Ask the realtor to see the home in the evening (or in the day if you have already seen it at night).
- Ask your realtor for a Competitive Market Analysis (CMA) which is a brief report that outlines how much similar homes have sold for, and prices for homes currently for sale. This will assist you in determining how much to offer for the home.
- Determine privately how much you are prepared to offer to purchase the home and reduce it somewhat to give yourself some negotiating room.
- Advise your realtor to prepare your offer — remember to stay calm!

What can happen after you make the offer? The best news would be that your offer is accepted. Or, the seller might make a counteroffer. If you receive a counteroffer, you have three choices:

- Accept the counteroffer, which usually means paying a higher price.
- You can issue a second counteroffer to the seller to hopefully arrive at a price between your first offer and the counteroffer from the seller.
- You can walk away and look for another home.

What happens if you lose the home? First of all, this is not uncommon. Don't feel bad and don't feel under pressure to buy the first or second home you like. There are always many homes for sale. In fact, the experience that you just went through is invaluable; it is something you can't learn in school. If you lose the home, it's time to move back to Step 7 — looking at homes and eventually making an offer to purchase another home which is accepted by the seller.

Step 9: Finalizing your home purchase and closing the deal

Your realtor will coordinate the closing details with you. That being said, there are a few things that will require your attention:

- Choose a lawyer or a title agency that will represent you on the closing. I suggest that you request quotations for fees and disbursements for three reputable firms and then select one. This will also assist you with your final budget of costs.
- Meet with your mortgage broker or lender and provide details of your accepted offer to purchase the home. Ask for a final "commitment letter," which confirms that the lender will issue the money for the home on the closing date.
- Wait until the conditions in your offer have been met. This would include the home inspection report, the appraisal, etc. Your realtor will then ask you to sign a form which confirms that all conditions have been met. Once signed by both you and the seller, the offer is no longer conditional and should close on the date agreed to. You have now bought the home!
- Review Step 3 and make arrangements for changes to utilities, and get quotations for moving costs, home insurance, appliances, and any other work you have planned.
- Your lawyer or title agency will call you to sign documents prior to the closing date. You may feel that you are signing your life away — there is a lot of paperwork! Fear not! It will be worth it when it is over.
- Assemble the money you have saved in preparation for the closing day.
- On closing day your title agency or lawyer will ask you to bring in a check for the amount owing to close the transaction. He or she will either give you the keys or advise you what time to pick them up.

After completing all the steps, you now own your first home — congratulations!

CHAPTER FIFTEEN

Tips for Couples

* Read this if you are currently in a serious relationship and wondering about moving in together.

* Read this if you are already living with your partner and are looking for tips to keep your finances and your relationship running smoothly.

* Read this if you are thinking of getting married and wondering about a traditional wedding versus a destination wedding.

Last time we saw Cassie she was calling her grandmother looking for the comfort of her wisdom. If anyone could help Cassie with advice on choosing a mate, Gram was the one.

After a long tight hug from Gram, Cassie begins to talk about Matt, Sam, and her dilemma. First Cassie describes Matt; how good natured and fun loving he is. Matt is everyone's best friend, he would lend his worst enemy $5 and not expect to get it back. Matt is generous with his time and his resources. Recently Matt has taken a new position as a sales rep with a wine wholesaler. This new position offers much more security and income. Matt could make a lot of money if he follows the career path available to him. Life with Matt would be full of adventure. She knows that Matt loves her dearly and would do anything to please her.

Gram interrupts, "OK Cassie, I hear a *but* coming up. What is it?"

"The truth is Matt is my best friend and we can talk about everything, but I worry about his approach to life. Matt believes in going with the flow. Recently he has been making plans for the future but most of the time he seems to prefer to just wing it. It makes me nervous, especially when it comes to money. We just seem to be in such a different place when it comes to planning for the future. I wonder if it will cause problems later on."

Gram asks, "Do you know how he is doing financially?"

Cassie admits that Matt has had difficulty in the past staying within his means and a recent accident meant he had to add debt to his charge cards, which already had a balance owing. "It's just like him to carry debt, and I have worked very hard to pay off my student loans as fast as I could. You taught me to watch every penny and I do. If I were to marry Matt, I would worry about our finances and be afraid that I might look like the big bad cop if we get into arguments about money."

Gram asks about Sam, which Cassie explains that Sam is different from anyone she has ever met. "He is charming and easygoing. Behind his easygoing manner lays a brilliant and strategic mind. Sam plans everything 5, 10, even 15 years in advance. He is focused and committed. When Sam sets his mind to something, no matter how small or large, you can count on him to complete the task. With Sam, I would know where we stood all the time. Life with Sam would be predictable, safe, and secure."

Gram asks, "How is Sam doing financially?"

Cassie tells Gram about Sam and his five-year plan, and how he is careful with his money. He put himself through school by working part time and keeping his grade average high enough to qualify for scholarships. Sam is content to drive a beat up old pick-up truck and live in a modest apartment if it means he can pay off his remaining student loans and further his plans to run a successful practice. Sam is comfortable taking a calculated risk if he can clearly see the payoff.

After some thought, Gram says, "Cassie, you may be disappointed with my advice. I cannot make this decision for you. Choosing a life partner is a big decision. The biggest you will ever make. All I can say is, you will need to think this through very carefully. You need to know yourself and your partner very well before you decide to marry or live together."

"Both of these men seem to have wonderful personal characteristics. They are hardworking and ambitious. In my experience the ambitious person succeeds more often than the educated one. Sam is educated and ambitious. He also has what in the old days was called character; the ability to forgo short-term wants to achieve important goals. Matt may have had a slow start but it sounds like he is beginning to discover his potential and ambitions. Matt will soon meet luck. Luck is what happens when diligence meets opportunity and it sounds to me that Matt is very good at creating his own luck. As long as he is able to get a handle on his finances he could make a good partner. If he does not begin to live within his means, your life together could be full of misery. At the end of the day you will have to rely on your instincts and common sense."

1. How to Reconcile Your Money Management Differences

There is no single decision you will make which will have a greater impact on your happiness and financial well-being than the choice of a life partner. It is beyond the scope of this book to provide advice on choosing a mate. The most important decision of your life is, "Who will I spend the rest of my life with?" Or in this age of divorce and remarriage, at least a good part of your life. Trust me when I say divorce is very painful, costly, and a big business where the only ones who win are the lawyers. With disagreements about money issues being among the top reasons couples separate, it make sense to have the money conversation before you decide to marry or live together.

Regardless of who you choose as your life partner, you will need to be able to communicate openly and learn to solve problems together. Couples need not have the same money style but they do need to know each other's money habits and have a plan for addressing each other's differences. Sharing common goals, adhering to a budget, and agreeing on who pays for what and how much will help both of you to reach an agreement before problems arise.

Begin by sharing. I am not talking about your toothbrush, tuna sandwich, or the car; I am talking about your financial history and your money styles. Before you make the decision to move in with your loved one, sit down together and talk about each other's financial status, history, and how you approach financial decisions. Doing so will provide both of you with a basis of forming future financial decisions as a team. This means a thorough understanding of current income, job stability, net worth, expenditures, financial obligations, and, most importantly, debt. If this seems like an awkward conversation to have, just try to think of the consequences of *not* having the conversation before you commit. The awkward conversation you don't have today will become increasingly difficult to introduce once you have an established relationship.

By sharing your financial stories, you and your partner will gain an appreciation for your money styles and deepen your feelings of intimacy and trust. Your ability to speak about money will mark you as a couple that is committed to the relationship and willing to work for the common good. It is an oddity of our modern culture that so many partners are willing to share the stories of their past romantic relationships, yet know nothing about each other's financial history.

If your prospective partner does not want to disclose his or her financial situation, you will need to ask yourself why. What is he or she hiding? Honestly ask yourself, "Do you want to share your life with a partner who keeps secrets?" I would suggest this type of partner is not ready for a committed relationship.

2. Solutions for Who Pays for What

Once you have shared your net worth and cash flow statements you will be in a good position to discuss how you will share future expenses. If you are working with a financial planner, this may be a good time to call him or her and book an appointment. Your financial planner can be counted on to be objective, and his or her advice will help you to work through your joint goals and budget. A financial planner can also help you to address issues you may not have thought about before, such as life insurance, wills, and powers of attorney.

Ask your partner the tooth fairy question: "What did you do with the money the tooth fairy left you?" Interestingly for many of us, our money style may not have changed much from the days when we believed in the tooth fairy.

Conflicts can arise when you and your partner approach money management with different money styles.

- One partner may feel perfectly comfortable knowing he or she has $50 in the bank, while the other's "feel-good" amount exceeds $1,000.

- You hate debt, but your partner is comfortable with debt.

- You want to start saving for a deposit on a home; your partner wants to take an expensive vacation this year and the next.

- Who pays for what, and who will keep track of the bills and bank balances?

All of these subjects should be discussed early on. It is a good idea to acknowledge that each of you may have different styles. With love, respect, and affection for each other you can be confident of reaching an amicable solution. Open communication will help both of you to understand each other's perspective and come up with a happy compromise.

Do you recall playing a game of tug-of-war as a child? To avoid conflicts about who pays for what, the two of you will need to select a cost-sharing formula. There are many ways to share expenses. The following sections include a few examples for you and your partner to consider. Choose the system which works best for you.

2.1 Pool all the money into one account

All money earned by you and your partner is deposited into a single account, and all expenses are paid from this account. All charge cards are entered jointly. All assets are owned jointly. You may recognize this method as the one your parents used while you were growing up. Indeed they may still use this method today.

There are advantages to pooling your money.

- This method offers the most transparency, as each partner sees exactly what goes into the account and what comes out.

- Each partner is valued as an equal contributor despite the actual number of dollars contributed.

There are definitely disadvantages to pooling money which belongs to you and your partner:

- All financial decisions become joint decisions. There is no room for privacy or independent spending by either individual.

- Requires the highest level of ongoing communication. While one of you is paying the dentist, the other may be writing a check for the car repair leading to an overdraft in your bank account.

- This method does not work when one partner is a spendthrift or uses the charge cards indiscriminately and adds to the couple's debt level.

2.2 Equal contribution

The equal-contribution method of cost sharing requires each partner to contribute the same dollar amount to a joint account each month. It ignores a discrepancy in how much each partner earns and assumes that when it comes to joint expenses, equal payment is fair.

The advantages of equal contribution include:

- Each shares equally in paying the bills and other communal costs.

- This method is easy to track. For example, if $100 comes out of your joint account, each of you adds $50.

The disadvantages of equal contribution include:

- Couples do not always earn a similar amount of dollars. Even if you begin earning the same amount, over time, one of you may lose your job while your partner receives a promotion.

- The partner with the lower income may become frustrated by trying to keep up with the lifestyle of the higher income earner. Indeed the lower income earner may have no discretionary money of his or her own.

- The partner with the higher income may become frustrated that he or she cannot do as much as he or she can afford to do, because his or her partner is not able to keep up.

This method may be equal, but it may not be viewed as fair.

2.3 Contribute a proportional percentage of earnings

Contributing a proportional percentage of earnings requires a couple to devise a budget that is within their means. They sit down with their partner and calculate how much money is coming in each month and then calculate the percentage each partner makes. For instance, you make $60,000 a year and your partner makes $40,000 a year. Your contribution to your joint accounts would equal 60 percent while your partner contributes 40 percent.

The advantages to this method:

- This is the fairest method of dividing expenses because each of you contributes according to your ability.

- Once you calculate the proportion of earnings, this method is easy to adhere to.

- Each partner has a remainder of money for his or her own discretionary expenses.

The disadvantage to this method is that it takes a bit of maintenance. It needs to be updated regularly as income changes.

2.4 Keep separate accounts

In this method, each of you keeps their separate accounts and negotiates who will pay for what. This may take the form of, "I will pay for the rent if you pay the car expenses and the groceries." Some couples have one partner pay for all of the "needs" (fixed-monthly operating costs) while the other partner pays for all of the "wants" (out-of-pocket cash and credit card items).

There are several advantages to keeping separate accounts:

- You both keep separate bank accounts; this means you each retain a measure of privacy and independence.

- If you do not share with one another about each other's debt obligations, you have a measure of protection from your partner's creditors. This method is desirable for situations when one partner enters into the relationship with high debt and/or a poor credit history.

- This method works for couples where one or both partners have financial obligations from a previous relationship (e.g., child support payments).

- Money earned that is not allocated to the couple's expenses can be used to reduce individual debt or increase savings.

The disadvantages to keeping separate accounts include:

- The split of expenses may not be fair, or if it is fair, for a short period of time it may become unfair when one partner has to take on new expenses (e.g., day care for a child or the cost of a second vehicle).

- Trying to renegotiate a split of costs later in your relationship may lead to quarrels.

3. Planning for Happiness While Protecting Yourself

While all couples plan for happiness, it is still a good idea to protect your assets and your credit score. If you are planning to, or are already living with a partner whose money style you are unfamiliar with, avoid sharing debt for now. Wait until you know each other's money style. Do not open a joint bank account and use a cost-sharing method of keeping separate accounts for now (see section **2.4**). Keep your own credit cards. Do not sign for joint charge cards, vehicle loans, or any loans for that matter. Protect your credit rating.

If you already have a joint account and charge cards and find they are being abused, talk to your partner. If this does not work, talk to your banker and have your name removed from the accounts. Tell your partner what you have done and that you will pay your fair share from your own account. If your name was on a joint charge card or loan, your banker will hold you responsible for any debt that was added to the accounts while you name was on the account.

It is equally important to know that you are not responsible for your partner's debt where you were not a joint owner of the account, credit card, loan, or utility (e.g., cell phone).

If you own your own home, make yourself familiar with the *Family Law Act* or an equivalent law in your area. It is important for you to know that your partner may have a legal claim to your home if you have lived together for some time. Note that the time could be as little as one year.

If you are having problems due to your partner's spendthrift ways and abuse of debt, you may need help. A good place to start is by calling your financial planner who can help you source out the appropriate professional in your neighborhood who can help you.

4. Getting Married

If you are planning a wedding, you are planning for one of the most exciting events of your lifetime. Each culture and nation has its unique traditions, but what they all have in common is a tradition for celebrating the marriage of a couple. As such, this may be one of the most expensive days of your life. Costs for a wedding reception can vary widely. It is not unusual for a dinner reception that includes alcohol to cost several hundreds of dollars per guest. Costs for a brunch or lunch can be expected to be somewhat lower. The good news is the cost of wedding celebrations is traditionally shared by the families.

Traditional weddings are popular with young couples who may not have already lived together but come from a cultural background where the role of a wedding is to start the young couple off on solid financial footing. For these lucky couples, the cost of a wedding can be quickly offset by the gifts they receive.

A popular choice for today's couples is the destination wedding. They choose a tropical destination, book a block of hotel rooms, and invite friends and family to join them. This is a good choice for couples who marry later in life, have been living together for some time already, and who wish to avoid the fuss and stress of a traditional wedding.

4.1 Talk to your parents

Some parents have set aside savings just for this event. Make no mistake: When children marry it is a big deal for the parents. You are probably unaware of their plans for your wedding. They may have set aside a few thousand dollars to either pay for a wedding or to use as a wedding gift. Talking to your parents about this in advance will give you a better idea of what you can expect.

While having this conversation, it is important to remember you are talking to your parents about a *gift*. Be respectful of your parents' wishes and their own financial circumstances. Start by telling them that whatever their plans, you are grateful for their help and respectful of their right to decline a discussion on this topic at this time.

As you discuss your plans with each set of parents, recognize that you and your partner's parents may not have the same financial resources or values. It is okay for each set of parents to provide differing levels of support. Again, please remember these are *gifts*. Contributions of differing amounts should not be seen as an occasion for complaint.

You may have some questions, the answers to which will help you to better plan for your future.

- Are your parents able and willing to assist financially with your wedding?

- What role would they like to play?

- If they plan to assist in your wedding plans, how much and under what conditions?

- Would part of your wedding gift be in the form of cash?

- Can you use these funds for a down payment on a home instead?

- If you choose not to marry, or do not marry before a certain age, what happens to the wedding account funds?

Once you know what to expect in the way of family support, it is time for you and your partner to work together on a budget for a realistic wedding plan that will not put you or your parents in debt.

Whatever your wedding plans, from a garden party for 30 people to 500 guests at The Ritz, you and your guests, family, and parents will be happiest if you establish and stick to a budget everyone can afford.

Conclusion

O ne thing is certain as you set out on your financial life plan; whatever your financial goal, when you take charge of your finances you will feel better about yourself and happier with your results. By establishing goals and developing a long-range strategy to achieve your goals, you will be amazed at the results that can be achieved in one short decade.

Imagine yourself ten years from today. Now ask your ten-year-older self: "If I were age 20 again, what would I do differently?" TD Canada Trust asked Generation X (ages 31 to 45) this very question:[1]

- 93 percent of respondents said they would have saved more money every month.

- 91 percent said they would have paid off more debt.

- 79 percent wished they had opened a retirement savings account.

This same poll found young adults relied on two sources for their financial advice:

- 26 percent said they relied on their financial advisor.

- Parents were a close second with dads at 24 percent and moms at 11 percent.

Never be afraid to ask for help from someone close to you who is willing and able to show you the way.

---

[1] TD Canada Trust, "Smart advice from Gen X to Gen Y: 'Save more now,'" http://smr.donovangroup.ca/TDBank/TDGetSaving.html, (October 6, 2010), accessed June 2011.

I hope you enjoyed meeting Cassie, Matt, and Sam in this book. Each has a different view on life and finances and just maybe you saw a little of yourself in one of them. All three are going to do just fine.

Cassie, in spite of the fact her earnings will continue to be modest, will become a millionaire before age 65. She will do so by living within her means and building her savings. We are not sure who she will choose to marry, but we are confident in her ability to make the right choice.

Matt has ambition and can spot opportunity when he sees it. He is on his way to an amazing career where he will have above-average earnings. I have met people like Matt before, who achieve extraordinary results with a combination of people skills, hard work, and a willingness to do whatever it takes. It would not be surprising to see him rise to the top echelons of his industry. Matt will enjoy an affluent lifestyle. If he learns to control his appetite for "wants" and begins to save for his future, he will become wealthy.

Sam has it all. He's a strategic thinker by nature so he cannot help but do well. Like a straight arrow, he intuitively takes the shortest distance between his current location and his desired destination. Sam understands the advantages of delayed gratification, making small sacrifices today to secure a better tomorrow. By avoiding bad debt and making use of good debt, Sam's wealth is already growing. We could all learn a little about financial planning from Sam.

It is my hope that the advice in this book plays a small part in your future happiness. The financial foundation you build today will carry you through your 30s and beyond. Goal setting, budgeting, reducing debt, and saving a portion of your income will all become habits that will lead to success.